hiking

ARIZONA

Urban Trails, Easy Paths & Overnight Treks

text and photography by contributors of
Arizona Highways Magazine

ARIZONA HIGHWAYS
BOOKS

front cover: Arizona's wild horizons and colorful vistas are within easy reach of casual hikers and adventurous backpackers, like these two at sunset. DON B. STEVENSON
(Detail, left to right) Arching arms of giant saguaro cacti. JACK DYKINGA
Red-spotted purple butterfly in Ramsey Canyon. JIM HONCOOP
Engelmann's prickly pear cactus blossom. JACK DYKINGA
inside front cover: Two hikers ascend a ridge in the Painted Desert. TOM BEAN
back cover: (Top) A ghoulishly draped chain fruit cholla cactus points toward the west face of the Superstition Mountains. GEORGE H.H. HUEY
(Middle) Hikers in Painted Desert. TOM BEAN
(Bottom) Snow drifts shelter a climber's tent in view of Humphrey's Peak. ROBERT G. McDONALD

ARIZONA HIGHWAYS
B O O K S

Book Designer: BILLIE JO BISHOP
Photography Editor: RICHARD MAACK
Book Editor: EVELYN HOWELL

Published by the Book Division of *Arizona Highways*® magazine, a monthly publication of the Arizona Department of Transportation, 2039 West Lewis Avenue, Phoenix, Arizona 85009.
Telephone: (602) 712-2200
Web site: www.arizonahighways.com

FIRST PRINTING, 2002.

Publisher: WIN HOLDEN
Managing Editor: BOB ALBANO
Associate Editor: EVELYN HOWELL
Associate Editor: PK PERKIN McMAHON
Art Director: MARY WINKELMAN VELGOS
Photography Director: PETER ENSENBERGER
Production Director: CINDY MACKEY

Printed in Korea

Library of Congress Catalog Number 2001092845
ISBN 1-893860-79-5

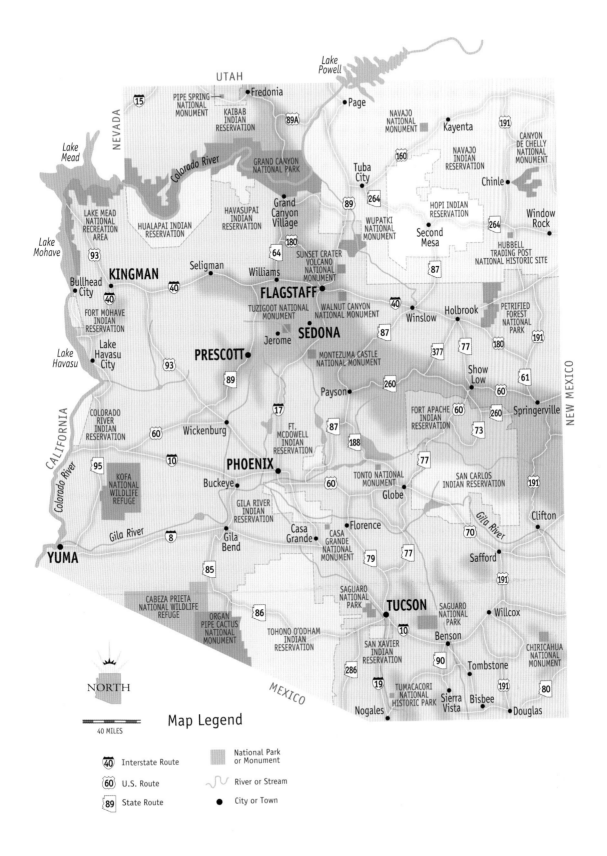

UTAH

NEVADA

Lake
Powell

15 PIPE SPRING
NATIONAL
MONUMENT
KAIBAB
INDIAN
RESERVATION

Fredonia

89A

Page

NAVAJO
NATIONAL
MONUMENT

Kayenta

191

CANYON
DE CHELLY
NATIONAL
MONUMENT

Lake
Mead

Colorado River

GRAND CANYON
NATIONAL PARK

160

NAVAJO
INDIAN
RESERVATION

Chinle

LAKE MEAD
NATIONAL
RECREATION
AREA

HAVASUPAI
INDIAN
RESERVATION

Tuba
City

89

264

Window
Rock

Lake
Mohave

HUALAPAI INDIAN
RESERVATION

Grand
Canyon
Village

WUPATKI
NATIONAL
MONUMENT

HOPI INDIAN
RESERVATION

264

93

Seligman

Williams

180

64

SUNSET CRATER
VOLCANO
NATIONAL
MONUMENT

Second
Mesa

HUBBELL
TRADING POST
NATIONAL HISTORIC SITE

Lake
Mohave

KINGMAN

40

FLAGSTAFF

WALNUT CANYON
NATIONAL MONUMENT

87

NEW MEXICO

Bullhead
City

FORT MOHAVE
INDIAN
RESERVATION

TUZIGOOT NATIONAL
MONUMENT

40

Winslow

Holbrook

PETRIFIED
FOREST
NATIONAL
PARK

40

SEDONA

87

191

Lake
Havasu
City

Jerome

377

77

180

Lake
Havasu

PRESCOTT

MONTEZUMA CASTLE
NATIONAL MONUMENT

Show
Low

61

93

89

260

Payson

60

260

Springerville

CALIFORNIA

COLORADO
RIVER
INDIAN
RESERVATION

60

Wickenburg

17

FT.
McDOWELL
INDIAN
RESERVATION

87

FORT APACHE
INDIAN
RESERVATION

73

95

10

188

77

191

KOFA
NATIONAL
WILDLIFE
REFUGE

PHOENIX

Buckeye

60

TONTO NATIONAL
MONUMENT

Globe

SAN CARLOS
INDIAN RESERVATION

Clifton

Colorado River

Gila River

GILA RIVER
INDIAN
RESERVATION

Casa
Grande

Florence

70

Gila River

8

YUMA

Gila
Bend

CASA
GRANDE
NATIONAL
MONUMENT

79

77

Safford

85

191

CABEZA PRIETA
NATIONAL WILDLIFE
REFUGE

86

SAGUARO
NATIONAL
PARK

TUCSON

SAGUARO
NATIONAL
PARK

Willcox

ORGAN
PIPE CACTUS
NATIONAL
MONUMENT

TOHONO O'ODHAM
INDIAN
RESERVATION

10

Benson

CHIRICAHUA
NATIONAL
MONUMENT

NORTH

286

SAN XAVIER
INDIAN
RESERVATION

19

90

Tombstone

191

80

MEXICO

Nogales

TUMACACORI
NATIONAL
HISTORIC PARK

Sierra
Vista

Bisbee

Douglas

Map Legend

40 MILES

40 Interstate Route

60 U.S. Route

89 State Route

National Park
or Monument

River or Stream

City or Town

contents

In the 14 years since *Arizona Highways* magazine published its hiking guide, Arizona has boomed with families, those who visit and those who move here. Hikers also have seen the dream of the Arizona Trail gradually come true. *Arizona Hiking: Urban Trails, Easy Paths and Overnight Treks,* a newly expanded hiking guidebook, highlights the Arizona Trail and combines exciting long-distance treks with a variety of shorter outdoor jaunts ideal for vacationing young families and enthusiastic beginners.

Why mix challenging backpacking trips with casual family outings? We think that one is not exclusive of the other. If you've never hiked in Arizona before, even if you've hiked long trails elsewhere, the climate and terrain here might still surprise you. The aridity, temperature changes and extremes, remoteness, and ruggedness that hikers find here demand awareness and conditioning. Reading is just a small step toward that awareness. Sampling small chunks of trails in a smorgasbord of terrains will be even more rewarding in building familiarity and competence. Besides, easier day hikes in Arizona do not skimp on natural bonuses: breathing fresh air, spotting wildlife, and stretching your legs amidst astounding beauty.

Arizona Hiking offers challenges to tantalize the hardiest hiker and building-block day hikes to satisfy adventuresome souls of all capabilities. If your goal is the journey, not just the final destination, there is much to savor even on the easiest of these trips.

We encourage you to get out and enjoy the outdoors — safely. The authors have described only those areas they personally hiked. However, conditions can change rapidly. To ensure your maximum enjoyment, please check ahead regarding current trail and environmental conditions, permit and fee status, fire regulations, and drinking water availability. (Wherever you decide to hike in Arizona, always assume that each person will need to take at least a gallon of drinking water for each day of the hike.)

Our thanks to Arizona authors John Annerino, Peter Kresan, and James E. Cook for their active contributions in *Outdoors in Arizona: A Guide to Hiking and Backpacking.* Their hiking, writing, and willingness to share their expertise is the foundation for this expanded version. And thanks to Wesley Holden, the *Arizona Highways* book editor (now retired) who first guided *Outdoors in Arizona* into print in 1987.

The additional hikes first appeared in *Arizona Highways* as the feature "Hike of the Month." For those of you who have asked when will we start compiling the hikes into book form, the answer is "Now." We thank the many authors who have vividly created in the mind's eye the outdoors that they've enjoyed first hand: Robert Albano, Peter Aleshire, Kathleen Bryant, Tom Dollar, Rick Heffernon, Rose Houk, Douglas Kreutz, Tom Kuhn, Christine Maxa, Sam Negri, Scott Parrish, James Tallon, Norm Tessman, and Bob Thomas. May their experiences — and their passion for Arizona's wild beauty — inspire you.

— THE *Arizona Highways* BOOK DIVISION

opposite page:
Beyond the threatening bristles of these teddy bear cholla, the dark cleft of Palm Canyon splits the Kofa Mountains.
JACK DYKINGA

There is a simple reason why Arizona is a hiker's paradise. It is space — the state's generous endowment of lands held in trust by the federal and state governments. There is ample room to roam and to explore because more than half of Arizona's land mass is owned by all of us, and we are free to enjoy it without being challenged as trespassers.

The essence of the well-publicized Arizona lifestyle is the incredible array of outdoor recreation options offered by the spacious people-to-land ratio available to us. Every time I ponder that almost 5 million Arizonans share close to the same number of square miles as 58 million Italians — and remember that states such as Texas and Iowa have only a few sparse acres of public lands — I glory in the wide-ranging outdoor recreation opportunities we have in the Southwest.

Among the most respected — and oldest — of such opportunities is trail hiking. This book is a splendid sampler for anyone interested in hiking Arizona's trails. The text in this guidebook begins in the backyards of our big cities, ranges over stretches of our singular desert terrain, leads us across some of our scenic mountains, and tours a select few of Arizona's canyons — with a climax walk into the Grand Canyon itself.

The diversity of Arizona's outdoor estate makes it a walker's wonderland:

- to savor in winter. Our state has some of the most interesting desert environments in the United States — including two of the largest low-desert wildlife refuges (Kofa and Cabeza Prieta) in America.

- to enjoy in all seasons. Arizona has a belt of pine-clad mountains which encompass the world's largest ponderosa pine forest and embrace unusual mountain "islands" rearing their refreshing ramparts in the southern part of the state.

opposite page: As perfectly stylized a plant as any cartoon animator could ask, the giant saguaro cactus is actually a tree with spines instead of leaves — leaves are too vulnerable to drought. The saguaro typically symbolizes Arizona, because its natural U.S. range is almost exclusively limited to this state.
JACK DYKINGA

- to wander over any time. There are remote wilderness areas in places such as the Gila Box and the Arizona Strip, where hikers seeking solitude can find untrammeled patches of beautiful land.
- to explore an astonishing array of canyons. Arizona calls itself "The Grand Canyon State," but rugged walkers quickly discover that the hundreds of large and small canyons crisscrossing every part of the state are its most dominant geographical feature.

Moreover, the Arizona earth is a "book" which contains special chapters for those with ecological interests. The Grand Canyon itself is, of course, the incomparable classroom for geologists. Birders who want to study one of the widest arrays of birdlife in the United States congregate in southern Arizona. Botanists can have a field day almost anywhere in the state, and our region has long been a mecca for amateur archaeologists and anthropologists interested in the cultures of the American Indian.

Some of Arizona's finest — and most inaccessible — wild and scenic lands are owned and protected by Indian tribes. Arizona has within its borders a higher proportion (27 percent) of Indian-owned land than any other state in the union. Fortunately, most tribes make part of their land available for outdoor recreation to non-Indians willing to pay appropriate fees and observe tribal and conservation regulations.

Among the most valuable tips in this primer about Arizona hiking are the descriptions of the day hikes available to the residents of our largest cities. To me, nothing adds more to the Arizona lifestyle than the opportunity offered to metropolitan parents to get their kids on nearby nature trails at young ages.

In this respect, Tucson has an unexcelled outdoor environment. It is the only large U.S. city bordered on two sides by a national park (Saguaro National Park) and on two other sides by areas that are part of our national system of wilderness lands. Venturesome Tucsonans can take a lunch and plenty of water, leave home on foot, spend the day in some of the nation's choice wild lands, and return at nightfall.

To me, walking is the best pastime there is. It is free, and it induces us to burn up our own calories, not irreplaceable hydrocarbons. It is, medical experts tell us, the best exercise in which we can engage. It also is a form of recreation where each person can set his or her own pace. And, if we open our senses to nature's sights and sounds, such excursions offer each of us precious tranquil moments when our home, that we call the earth, can whisper wisdom in our ears.

— STEWART L. UDALL

Born to pioneer parents in the small eastern Arizona town of St. Johns, attorney Stewart L. Udall has long been a conservationist and outspoken advocate for America's wild and natural lands — as congressman, Secretary of the Interior, and private citizen.

The richest values of wilderness lies not in the days of Daniel Boone
nor even in the present but rather in the future.
— ALDO LEOPOLD, American forester, author, and ecologist (1887-1948)

A successful trip into the wilderness does not require being in top shape, using high-tech gear, or traveling to the farthest edges of the earth.

It does require that you simply get out there.

Backcountry travel has as many variations as cooking, music, or driving. You might carry a 60-pound pack and trek for nine days or a tight, 20-pound pack and go for two weeks. You may never go overnight in your life, choosing day hiking without a cumbersome pack, just as you may prefer a backcountry entrée of fresh asparagus in hollandaise sauce lightly dusted with paprika — or two generous handfuls of nuts and raisins for dinner. However you choose to go out there, it is merely important that you do it.

There is something indefinably different about the natural world beyond the streets and sidewalks of civilization. The wilderness does not lack complexity or difficulty, but it is quick to reveal its rhythms.

If you don't know what I mean, step outside one night, just out the front door. Hold your hand against the sky long enough for the stars to move between your fingers. Now you know.

Discover that difference in the scatter of forest leaves, stacks of water-driven cobbles, the passage of clouds. If you go out there, it will be inevitable. So find the place and go.

Beginning the Journey

There are many different ways of tramping through Arizona's outdoors. If you're a beginner, which is the best place to be — you'll likely see things that old-hat hikers no longer spot — you'll cultivate your own style over time. Use your head, and your level of experience will generally dictate how far you can go and what places you can reach. Remember that a 20-year desert veteran may be just a beginner when hiking alpine trails. Each region has its own character, its own dangers and pleasures.

If you're a novice traveling with experienced people, they'll likely unload volumes of instruction. Swallow what they say — even this introduction —with a grain of salt. Others' experiences can be a good teacher, but don't believe that there is only one way to do things in the backcountry. There is never just one way. Even among experts who roam for most months of the year, opinions differ widely on how to load a pack, what to do with human waste, how to build a fire, what fabrics to wear.

Start slowly. Try the desert for a day or two. Get up into the mountains for an afternoon and savor the change in elevation. Walk into northern Arizona's canyons or through the oak grasslands near the southeast border with Mexico. Trails give a good starting point because they go to known destinations, and you don't have to worry incessantly about where to put your next step — assuming trail maintenance is up to date. Discover your body's parameters — how far you can go, how fast, how slow. Where do you get blisters most often? Did you run out of water last time?

Covering huge distances of backcountry as fast as you can is not the best goal. Get back somewhere, away from other people, and try walking as slowly as possible. I mean s-l-o-w-l-y. Take 10 minutes to cover 100 feet, and look at everything around you. Hiking is not just the measure of your physical exertion, but a fresh chance to savor a different world. Experiment more, rush less.

After some day trips, try staying out overnight if it seems fitting and if you have the right gear — sleeping bag, raincoat, some appropriately warm or cool clothes, and a pack that will hold it all.

Or you may want to start swiftly — head right into a weekend backpacking trip. You'll quickly figure out what works for you and what doesn't. You might be uncomfortable under too much weight in your pack or with too little warmth at night. Maybe you'll discover, as your muscles cramp, that you need more physical conditioning. Either way, assuming you made common-sense preparations and didn't take foolish risks, you'll probably survive and come back with a good idea of what to do next time.

If you remember anything from this introduction, remember this: Each place is different. Rules of behavior, survival, and enjoyment change from region to region. You will find that you must move differently in pristine, untrailed areas than you do in popular areas. Study each place you travel. Learn what works and what doesn't. Make mistakes, but use your head so that you can live to learn from them.

Finding the Place

So, where do you want to go? The easiest way to choose is through a book like this. If you like maps, have a look at them. Learn how to read a "topo" (a topographical

opposite page: Wading confidently through the narrows of Paria Canyon, this backpacker can rely on the preparations he made for the specific demands of this remote route. JACK DYKINGA

map) and explore the place with your eyes to see if you want to enter steep, difficult topography or open country.

Or you can foster an intimacy with a specific region over time. Go back to the same place over and over, each time exploring new directions and possibilities. At the Grand Canyon, start with a major thoroughfare — Bright Angel Trail or North Kaibab — then see where lesser, arterial trails lead to. Eventually, maybe after a few years and some strong experience, you'll find yourself far off trail on treks into strange, unseen places.

No matter where you travel in the Sonoran Desert, it will be beautiful. Any approach to the San Francisco Peaks will be mystifying. There is not just one perfect place.

above: In the Chiricahua Mountains, fingered by the November sun, the South Fork of Cave Creek curves under a canopy of brilliantly colored maple trees.
ROBERT G. McDONALD

Conditioning Your Body

If you choose the Grand Canyon, there will be certain constraints on your body. With 10,000 vertical feet going down one side and up the other, this place is physically difficult, and many people get rescued every year, delirious and exhausted. That doesn't mean you have to break your back whenever you travel the Grand

Canyon. If you are not in top shape for crossing from rim to rim, try one of the trails, like those across the Tonto Platform, where there is not so much up and down.

Having your body in shape for the hikes you do is important. Picking a hike that matches your body is equally important. Arizona has some dramatically rough landscapes. Know your body's limits, because some places are far more challenging than others. At the same time, if you qualify as a couch potato, don't let your sedentary state stop you. There's an outdoor experience to fit anyone's level of fitness. Your first hike may be more of a brief stroll, but at least now you're up and about and absorbing the wilderness world that lives beyond our living rooms and offices.

Learn basic stretches and practice them before going out. This helps avert injuries such as torn muscles. Keeping in good cardiovascular condition through jogging, steady walking, or other activities that raise your heart rate will help you avoid crumpling exhausted midway through a hike. If you'll be backpacking with a 30- or 40-pound pack, strengthen your back and shoulders.

Let's say you're set on hiking up 4,808-foot Mount Ajo in Organ Pipe Cactus National Monument in the early spring. Do shorter desert hikes to condition for the physical and environmental demands. If you'll hike the 12,000-foot-plus summits of the Kachina Peaks Wilderness, do shorter, high-altitude hikes, say on Kendrick Peak, to train for it. Try to plan your first couple of day hikes or overnighters in an environment where you're already physically and mentally comfortable.

Your training also should be well-rounded enough to deal with unexpected situations, like getting "turned around" and having to double your mileage to get back to your car. Even the best hikers get disoriented. As Daniel Boone once said, "I ain't never been lost before, but I've been in some mighty strange country for three or four days."

When on your hike, stay in tune with your body. Thirst is a poor indicator of fluid requirements. If you're thirsty, chances are that you're already dehydrated, so drink regularly and often. Your urine should be pale yellow, almost clear. If your urine starts to turn dark yellow, you need to stop exercising and replenish lost fluids with water. On the other hand, if your urine is clear *all day*, it means that you need to eat more. Hyponatremia is a dangerous condition that comes from ample water consumption, but not enough sodium, chloride, and calcium, which keeps the metabolism working. In case of hyponatremia, sit down in the nearest shade and eat.

Be smart. If you are not feeling well along your hike, stop. Think about what might be wrong. Don't just keep marching ahead. Tell the people hiking with you to sit down and wait if you are too tired. If they want to keep moving, tell them to sit down anyway and enjoy the view.

Expectations

The wilderness won't be what you expect, no matter how many years you've been out trekking. If you want sun, it will rain. If you want to see coyotes, you will see elk. If you want it to rain, it will snow. That is the wild beauty of these places. You cannot command them. The clouds will roll over you no matter how much you shout at them to go away.

If you head into the boonies with the attitude that nature is out to get you, or that you're going to "conquer" nature, you're going to have a fight on your hands — and there's no question who's going to get whipped.

You might hope this guidebook will tell you exactly where to go and what it will be like. No guidebook can tell you that; it's merely a list of suggestions and possible locations, a microscopic look at one person's experiences at a particular time and place. If the wilderness could be reduced to common definitions, it would no longer be wild.

As you explore, your expectations will only expand. Sometimes, seven days into a 30-day backpacking trip, I'll think that I've seen it all, that I know what this trip will be like. But by the 30th day, I'm nothing like who I was on the seventh day. The wilderness changes you, whether you cover 2,000 miles a year or go out for an afternoon every few weeks.

So take a little time, a few weeks before your first overnighter, and read about the area you're going to hike. Visualize what the area will be like. Once you're there, you'll already have laid important psychological groundwork to deal with problem situations.

If you're embarking on what to you is a long trek, and you start thinking about the entire hike, the scope may overwhelm you. Take it a manageable bit at a time, until you reach the next spring or ridgetop; soon you'll have put a series of those intermediate goals together.

Plan your trip for good conditions, but prepare psychologically for a worst-case scenario. Conditions in the wilderness can change suddenly and drastically. Your responses should be flexible and mature. Go as a student and learn what nature has to teach you. You may feel what naturalist John Muir felt: "Nature's peace will flow into you as sunshine flows into trees. The winds will blow their own freshness into you, and the storms their energy, while cares drop off like autumn leaves."

When to Go

Let the season be the indicator. If you're doing a desert backpack in the spring, start at daybreak and hike until mid-morning, take a siesta in the shade during the warmest part of the day, and resume hiking mid-afternoon. However, if you're doing a winter mountain hike, you'll probably want to sleep in and start your hike when things warm up, stop for lunch, hike through the afternoon, and make camp long before the sun sets.

For instance, you probably wouldn't enjoy hiking Aravaipa Canyon during late fall or winter. The days are short and the air is cool, so wading back and forth across the creek is unpleasantly cold and even dangerous. Better to go in late spring or early fall. There are exceptions to these general guidelines. Weigh environmental factors against your experience and physical capabilities before you decide when to do a particular hike.

What to Take

Outdoor Essentials — When going outdoors in Arizona, there are some survival basics to heed, whether you think you'll be away for just two hours or several nights: The key to staying warm is to first keep dry. If you are out walking for more than 15 minutes, always, always take plenty of water with you. Tell someone responsible where you're going and when you'll be back.

Here are some other tips to keep in mind. In the summer heat of deserts (or spring and fall, for that matter) it is often better to cover your skin with light cotton, rather than to be exposed directly to the sun. However, cotton is not good in cold and wet conditions, which can include sudden desert storms. Take a hat — it keeps your head warm in cold/wet/windy conditions and shades you in the heat.

Basic equipment — Whether you're on a desert day hike or an extended mountain backpack, basic gear includes: a good knife, pocket or sheath; "strike anywhere" matches in a water-proof container (small film canisters work well) or some small butane lighters; a small flashlight; and topographical maps folded and sealed in a zippered plastic sandwich bag, along with a pen. Most important, take something for carrying drinking water and some gear that will keep you warm and dry or protected from the sun.

Depending on environment and season, such gear means a sleeping bag and a tent or a waterproof bivvy bag. Tents or bivvies aren't always necessary, but if you haven't gone out often, it's much easier to set a tent or jump in a bivvy than to build a shelter with a tarp during a strong wind-and-rain storm at night. Not every tent is weatherproof. Some, especially ones with rain flies covering only the tops, will leave you quite damp in a heavy storm.

Sleeping bags — They're rated by temperature, which won't always mean that you'll be comfortable at that temperature. It might mean just that you'll live through the night and then go marching exhausted, cold, and cranky back to the trailhead come morning. People sleep well at different temperatures, so how you gauge a bag's performance will vary. If anything, use a bag rated for 20 degrees below the coldest night temperature you're expecting. Debating between down and synthetic fiber? Dry Arizona is a good location for using down bags, which tend to be lighter and stuff smaller than synthetic bags.

Clothes and shoes — Layering is easy and effective. Rather than wearing one heavy set of garments, take several light layers of clothing that are easy to doff or don as the weather and your body temperature change. Your minimum combination of layers should be comfortable during warmer stages of your hike, while still letting you add enough layers to stay warm when temperatures drop. Fabric choices can make subtle, unexpected differences; on a windy day, a light windbreaker over a light wool sweater may actually keep you warmer than one heavy jacket that got you damp and sweaty earlier in the hike. Cotton won't insulate you properly, especially if it's wet or cool and windy. Wool and some of the insulating synthetics do a much better job of keeping you warm.

For desert hiking, I'd take a well-broken-in pair of lightweight hiking shoes, with good traction and ankle support; cotton or light wool athletic socks; light-colored, loose-fitting cotton pants; a cotton T-shirt or long-sleeved cotton shirt; a cotton hat; and a good pair of sunglasses. Why long pants instead of shorts? One word — cactus. Well, make that two words — snakes. High-topped hiking shoes and

long pants give you better protection on both counts. Loose, volcanic rock is typical of desert hiking, so watch your step and wear shoes with ankle support.

If you're on an overnighter, and the season warrants, take a good wool watch cap, a warm jacket, and perhaps a change of socks. How much you take depends on how much you want to carry. Watch the ounces, and the pounds will take care of themselves.

For a wet canyon hike like in Aravaipa or Paria, keep a dry change of shoes and clothes in your pack. They'll make evenings much more comfortable.

For mountain hiking, depending on the season, you may need warm, snow-proofed boots; a pair of thick wool socks, lined with thin nylon socks to draw the moisture away from your feet; loose-fitting wool pants and shirt; wool sweater, wool gloves or mittens, and a wool hat; a down or fiberfill coat; dependable rainwear; a change of wool/blend or polypropylene underwear; and additional warm clothes carried in your pack.

Water — A gallon a day is the general rule for drinking water. Carrying a couple of quart water bottles and a larger collapsible water container do well, depending on where and when you go. If walking across Cabeza Prieta National Wildlife Refuge's desert in summer, you'll need to carry nearly two gallons per day. If you're following the Black River in the White Mountains, two quart bottles will see you easily from place to place because you won't dry out as quickly and there are natural water sources. It all depends on how much available drinking water is out there and how much water you'll need.

If you find a natural water source, do you fill your canteen? I say a qualified yes. The purest-looking stream, spring, or pool, however remote, almost certainly harbors troublesome microbes — bacteria, viruses, or parasites that can make you very sick — left by some animal, not necessarily man; however, that probably tainted trickle may be the only water at hand. (Hopefully, you've planned ahead and are never in this bind, but if you are . . .) You can use closely woven fabric, like a bandanna, to filter out mud and visible particles, but to guard against microorganisms, you'll need boiling, chemical disinfection, or portable filtration.

Given time and proper equipment, boiling water is the surest way to purify it. Boiling kills everything. Vigorously boil your drinking water for two to five minutes if you're near sea level; the higher up you are, the longer you'll need to boil it — say 15 to 20 minutes at 10,000 feet elevation — since water at high elevations boils at lower temperatures. Five to 10 minutes at 212° F. will kill both bacteria and viruses. This option becomes no option at all, though, if you're in wilderness where regulations prohibit a campfire.

Chlorine tablets, household bleach, and iodine tablets are all means for chemical disinfection, but they're not proven to kill all harmful protozoans. Commercially available tablets (check the sporting goods section of a department store or outdoor specialty shop) are relatively inexpensive and easy to use; just follow the package directions. If using household bleach, put in two drops per quart of water (four drops if water is cloudy). With 2 percent tincture of iodine, which may be in your first-aid kit already, use 10 drops per quart. Whatever you use, dissolve the chemical thoroughly in the water, which should then sit for at least 30 minutes before use. Also, with either iodine or chlorine, remember that large doses can be toxic; that potency generally declines with age; and that chemical effectiveness depends on water temperature and amount of organic material suspended in the water.

Portable filters come in such an assortment that you should be able to find one that's easy for you to carry and use. They're geared to filter out a considerable range of nasties for multiple uses, but the cheapest still costs considerably more than tablets do.

Food — Whether your tastes are gourmet or minimalist, there are supplies to suit everyone. Pack as light as possible, or porter a pantry's worth of ingredients for the ultimate dining experience under the stars. What matters is your enjoyment and physical well-being. Just be sure to have a good combination of proteins and complex carbohydrates to refuel your energy for your entire trip.

First aid — What you take depends on how much you know. If you don't know when or how to use it, will it help? At least include an antiseptic (iodine, Neosporin, etc.) for cleaning wounds and tweezers for removing splinters, cactus spines, and dirt from cuts. (A tip for cleansing a deep and dirty cut: In a plastic, sealable bag, mix water and a small amount of iodine; snip one corner at the bottom of the bag and squeeze, sending an irrigating stream of iodine water into your wound.) A small hair comb can remove large cactus spines. Gauze and adhesive tape are also good, whether for tending to blisters or covering an open gash. You can easily carry many other items in a first-aid kit, but these are basics.

Day Hikes — Check the information above to see what applies — at least a water bottle or two, perhaps a first-aid kit. Matches or a lighter are small, light, and very useful if you get stuck on the trail unexpectedly after dark.

Dangers

The backcountry is less dangerous than a city freeway, but there are certainly things to learn out here. Sometimes the best teacher is experience, assuming you survive to put the lessons into practice. This book is not a comprehensive survival guide. Rather than trying to train you to expertly cope with every possible catastrophe, this guide offers that ounce of prevention you can use to enjoy the wilderness safely. There are many good sources on backcountry survival practices (see Chapter 7).

When you picture your hike, what hazards do you imagine? If rattlesnakes are your biggest fear — well, they don't tend to pose much of a threat, but they are a natural feature of Arizona's wilderness. When hiking, you really should be most concerned about climate- or weather-related hazards: flash floods, dehydration, heat stroke, and hypothermia.

Every year, Arizona flash floods kill 10 to 30 people. July, August, and September are when you most need to beware. Look at the sky, and know where you are. If you're in a canyon or wash, where does the drainage begin? If it begins 30 miles away, you might not see the storm sending a flood your way. If your canyon is only a mile long, a flood will come only if the storm is right on top of you. In long canyons where you might not see the storm, keep track of exits, places where you can climb to safety at a moment's notice. Knee-high water can easily be fatal, no matter how well you swim. When it's moving fast and full of debris, water can be incomparably dangerous.

As a rule, don't drive across a wash or dip in the road when water is coming through. Every year, people stall in only 2 feet of water, then the water rises and carries the car away, four-wheel drive or not.

While watching for weather changes, remember to stay off ridgetops and open meadows during lightning storms. Unless you're an expert mountaineer, avoid the higher mountain peaks during heavy snows and winter storm warnings.

Arizona sun is strong, so cover your skin, either with cotton garments and/or sunscreen ointments. Shading your head with a hat or scarf is important (you may enjoy one you wet down for an evaporative-cooling effect). Drink plenty of water the day before you hike, so you don't start out already slightly dehydrated (you'll have to make more pit stops, but it's better than passing out on the trail). You know that you need to carry plenty of water, but if you run out of water in the summer desert, rest in the shade until sunset and travel at night. If you must travel during the day, go from shade to shade, or make some with a blanket or tarp. Reduce water loss through your mouth by avoiding panting and talking. Limit eating — or don't eat at all — if your water is low or has already run out. Besides the water you carry, keep some in your vehicle.

Hypothermia, "killer of the unprepared" and often called exposure, is the most insidiously dangerous of physiological hazards. You don't have to be high up a mountain to get hypothermia. It's a hazard to sea, desert, wilderness, and mountain survival. You can be in excellent shape, and the temperature doesn't have to be below freezing. In fact, hypothermia most often occurs in 30- to 50-degree air temperatures.

All it takes is inadequate or damp clothing and a cool breeze for the body to begin losing heat faster than it can replace it. Make that wet clothing from snow or cold-water immersion, and you go from the wind-chill factor to the wet-chill factor, which is even more dangerous. Your body temperature needs to drop only a degree or two to distinctly impair judgment and reaction time. Add in exhaustion, and people start doing very foolish things.

If you're caught in rain or snow, or just get very damp, get into dry clothes with good insulating values (wool rather than cotton). If only your feet are wet, get dry socks on. Don't let yourself get chilled to the point of shivering, because that's already an early stage of hypothermia. Even a chilly wind can make your temperature drop if you aren't wearing a protective layer to hold in body heat. Prevent hypothermia by knowing the symptoms, staying dry and out of the wind, wearing enough proper clothing, and keeping your head warm.

As the voice of reason, let me add that mine shafts and tunnels should be avoided for obvious reasons.

But you're still thinking about snakes, aren't you? Rattlesnakes don't tend to be very aggressive. Usually they'll rattle to tell you that they are there, then slide off into a crack or the grass to escape. The best place to find them is in thick ground vegetation; under, around, and in large logs; and tucked into rock cracks. If you don't put your hands and feet into places you can't see, you probably won't be bitten by a snake or other poisonous reptile. So when going over a large rock or log, it's better not to step over the obstacle in one stride. Why? On either side of the rock or log, your foot might wedge in near the base and disturb any crevice-lounging reptile. Instead, step up onto the log (or rock), then take a second step down on the other side, landing well clear of the base.

Use a stick to bat the brush ahead before your feet get there. If I think a rattlesnake might be in the grass ahead, I find a stick, beat it around, make sure there are no warning rattles, then walk through. At night in the desert, snakes like to sprawl on warm, flat ground and on asphalt, so use a light. Someone I know, who was bitten, was wearing sandals and stepped on a snake at night in open desert — one reason why long pants and boots are recommended for Arizona hiking, especially in brushy or desert areas.

Most people don't die from a rattlesnake bite. Those most at risk are the extremely young, the extremely old, and the allergic. However, it's still a painful injury. You'll probably read of several ways of dealing with venomous snakebites, with little agreement among doctors about which is best. You have to use your own judgment, but I would not cut open a rattlesnake bite and suck the venom out; because of the nature of the venom, I'd likely introduce an infection much worse than the bite itself.

Where does that leave you? If you do get bitten, stay as calm and still as possible. Accelerated heartbeat from anxiety or exertion pumps the venom faster. If possible, get to a hospital quickly. At least send someone for competent help. Ha! you say. I'm out in the middle of nowhere with a snakebite, and I'm supposed to get to the hospital quickly but without exerting myself? Chemically activated cold packs, available at drug stores, can slow down the venom's rate of travel. Apply the cold pack wrapped in a towel, shirt, or bandanna so that it doesn't freeze your skin. If you must hike out on your own, set a moderate pace; use meditation techniques, if you've practiced them, to lower stress; and remind yourself that this injury is not fatal. This particular exertion is necessary and helpful — panic is not.

If you get lost, sit down. People usually get hopelessly lost because they panic. They don't take a moment to piece their day back together mentally, to recall landmarks accurately. They keep moving, becoming more and more lost. So sit down. Relax. If you're going to be lost overnight, accept it. Find shelter, build a fire if you need one, and find your way back in the morning if you figure out where you are. It may be a long night, but it will make for a good story. If you don't know where you are, and people know that you're lost, stay put until they find you. It's easier for rescuers to search you out when you are not running away from them. When you get home, you'll remember that next time you'll pay more attention to the map, observe the landmarks and direction headings more, and stay on the trail.

Don't head into the bush thinking that somebody's always able to rescue you with a helicopter. In some areas and certain weather conditions, an expeditious rescue is next to impossible. Know your escape routes before you embark on a hike,

opposite page: Fall sunlight shimmies through the yellowing leaves of a Fremont cottonwood framed by the sharply cut cliffs of Aravaipa Canyon.
JACK DYKINGA

and don't burn any bridges if you have any doubts about your capabilities or the trail ahead.

Finally, don't rely on your gear more than you rely on yourself. If you depend solely upon a global positioning device to guide you back to your car, you might find the arrow pointing straight into a cliff face. The terrain is more complex than maps and devices. Stay alert. Know your limits. Go prepared.

Survival Reminders

Arizona's Camino del Diablo, the Devil's Highway, claimed the lives of many en route to California goldfields in the 1850s. Sheer hardiness and courage didn't always compensate for poor planning and 150 miles of waterless desert. Back then, you learned about survival the hard way.

Survival is not fun or easy, though some survival texts now tell us how to chuckle through all but the most dire situations if we use their elaborate techniques. Let's be realistic. When was the last time any of us caught a three-course brunch in a snare, trap, or deadfall? How many of us could start a fire with a crude bow drill? When was the last time you found any potable water somewhere as dry as the lower Sonoran Desert in midsummer?

Hopefully, none of us will ever have to learn, but as headlines every year point out, many ordinary folks are thrust into survival situations, whether by plane wreck, flat tire, or poor planning.

This is not expert survival training, just practical advice to help you avoid hard-core, primitive survival situations (see Chapter 7 for survival sources):

- Carry more water than you think you'll need.
- Don't hike in the heat of the day.
- Check ahead on all the water sources in the area you'll visit.
- Try to plan your camps to be near water — without risk of flash flooding.
- Know where you're going and where you are at all times in relation to the map you carry.
- Tell someone where you're going, the route you're taking, and when you'll be home.
- Check on the weather from more than one source.
- Don't overestimate your abilities.

Hiking Solo

The rule most often spoken is never go solo. I don't like this rule. If you want to go solo, then go. Just be smart about it.

Traveling alone is a completely different world than going with others. It is more dangerous, but if you change your behavior accordingly, you can minimize that danger: Take fewer risks; maybe let solitude be your adventure rather than clambering over rock falls. If you can, get to know a region well before you solo there. Even if you can't familiarize yourself in person, use a good map or two — a topo map to show the terrain and one that shows current roads, trails, and ranger stations. Identify major landmarks to help pinpoint directional headings.

opposite page:
Well-watered canyons may disclose secret gardens, like this bed of golden columbines growing along the West Fork of Oak Creek. JACK DYKINGA

Make sure people know where you're going, when you plan to return, even where you plan to park your vehicle. Tell them that, if you're not back by a certain day and time, they should call the authorities.

Hiking Techniques

You might think hiking is just putting one foot in front of the other. For the most part it is, but there are two techniques you'll find helpful. Going uphill you want to use the "rest step." Basically, take a short step with one leg, lock your knee, and take the next step, lock your knee, and so on. Locking your knee lets you rest on one leg while taking the next step.

When hiking downhill, use the "shuffle". Braking on every downhill step puts incredible strain on your ankle, knee, and hip joints, and it can make hiking exhausting and dangerous if you're walking along an exposed trail. The key to the shuffle is to relax your body and your leg muscles, so that your muscles — not your joints — absorb the shock of each step downhill. This also gives you a better feel for the trail. If you do start to slide on a ball-bearing type surface, you can control your descent easier. These techniques require some practice, but they'll make your hike easier.

Wilderness Ethics

For some reason, we like to put up markers, stabbing mountain summits with posts that can be seen from miles around, as if announcing that we've conquered something. Keep in mind that there is nothing to conquer out there. The mountains are going to stay for about 10 million more years than you, and a victory post will either fall over or be knocked down by the next people to come along with their own post.

Leaving our mark all over the place seemed fitting a hundred years ago when not many people were in remote locations. But now we mostly travel into the wilderness to find places unmarked by man. Make your motto that adage, "Take only photographs, leave only footprints."

In certain places I try not to leave even footprints. Maybe I do it so that if people come behind me, they might think they are the first to walk here. Maybe I do it just because the hard lines of my boot print seem out of place on the soft ground of a spruce forest or the sculpted sand of a desert wash.

What about campfires? Not every place allows campfires. Check with park or forest rangers about fire danger and current fire restrictions before setting out. Even when there are no seasonal restrictions, ask yourself whether you really need a fire and if it poses any danger to the environment (in desert environments, charcoal can easily last a few thousand years). Where allowed, campfires can be done effectively and without leaving scars.

If you do light a fire, here are some tips: Make a small fire, using only sticks on the ground that can be broken by hand. If you build a fire ring, avoid using volcanic rocks, which contain gases, and streambed rocks, which might hold moisture; heat can explode either kind. Carry a small fire pan; I've come to enjoy my pan, a thick

opposite page:
Protected wilderness areas, like Aravaipa Canyon, ask hikers to behave like careful guests — not rampaging intruders.
DAVID MUENCH

aluminum dish just a bit larger than a spread hand. By using a fire pan, you can move the fire from place to place and easily scatter the ashes in an exposed, weathering area such as a sandy wash the next morning. If you're in a popular location, use pre-existing fire pits. In a pristine area, don't make a fire pit at all. Mostly, don't make a fire unless you must.

Human waste? Bury it. If you dig below 6 or 8 inches, you're going too deep, getting below the biotic layer of efficient decomposition. Stay a couple hundred feet away from water sources such as streams, springs, or ponds. Carry out your toilet paper, or use it to start a camp fire that night. Or be radical, and try a few smooth, small river rocks and the freshly fallen leaves of non-poisonous plants. This procedure is delicate and not for everyone. But try it out sometime, it might not be that bad.

When you're out overnight, you might wonder where to set camp. Where many people have been, find an spot that's already flattened out. Try for more hardened ground — it is wonderful to sleep on open slick-rock. Don't camp in a wash — that's where water flows, hard and fast! Setting a solo or two-person camp, you can choose smaller, more intimate places than you can with groups. In some environments,

above: Desert terrain can look tough and impervious to human presence, but desert ecosystems, like this saguaro cactus forest in the Ajo Mountains, are remarkably fragile. Careless actions can easily damage their interconnected elements with lasting results.
GEORGE H.H. HUEY

especially where soil is soft, take sandals for walking in camp (they tear up the ground much less than the lugs of boots).

This isn't to say that people don't belong in the wilderness. We do belong there. Some think that we'd die as a civilization if we couldn't get out to the Middle-of-Nowhere at least once or twice a lifetime. But there are so many of us now tromping all over the place, that it is a good idea to start being a little more quiet and gentle about it.

The concept is simple, but in practice it can get a little detailed if you're not familiar with backcountry routines. Here are specific pointers for wilderness etiquette from the U.S. Forest Service's Backcountry Ethics.

Setting camp — Camp at least 300 feet from streams or springs. State law prohibits camping within a quarter mile of an only available water source (for wildlife and livestock). Don't cut trees, limbs, or brush to make camp improvements.

Breaking camp — Naturalize the area to look as if no one had been there. Replace rocks and wood used; scatter needles, leaves, and twigs on the site. Be sure you've left nothing behind. Everything you packed in should be packed out.

Campfires — Use gas stoves, when possible, to conserve firewood. If you must build a fire, use an existing fire ring. If you need to clear a new fire site, keep it small and in a safe spot — away from rock ledges that would be blackened by smoke; away from meadows where it would destroy grass and leave a scar; and away from dense brush, trees, and duff where it's a fire hazard. Put it cold out before leaving.

Trash — Carry out all trash, however small, that cannot be completely burned (aluminum foil, aluminum-lined packages). Don't bury trash; animals dig it up. (You might feel good packing out trash you find. A good example may catch on.)

Washing — Wash yourself, your dishes, and your clothes in a container. Food scraps, toothpaste, even biodegradable soap, pollute streams and springs. Pour wash water on the ground away from streams and springs.

Trails — Don't short-cut trails; it triggers erosion.

Structures and ruins — Leave gates, cabins, and other structures the way you find them. Federal law prohibits disturbing historic and prehistoric sites. Do not dig in sites or remove objects.

opposite page:
Their day opened before dawn at the foot of Squaw Peak. Now two hikers renew themselves with a sunrise meditation at the summit, high above a still-yawning Phoenix.
EDWARD McCAIN

To a frail city boy fresh off the streets of 1950s Chicago, the cinnamon-red humps of Phoenix's Papago Buttes were beyond civilization, a stark no-man's land.

If diamond-eyed rattlers didn't drag me to their dens, saber-tusked javelinas would munch on my spindly legs. For a 12-year-old, this ghastly picture of the Papago Buttes netherworld became a dare; the buttes were visible from my family's cinder-block "fortress." To tread that vastness and return alive became my obsession.

With a giant can of Franco-American spaghetti, my mother's wool comforter, and two GI canteens, I struck out along McDowell Road toward this great unknown. How long before I'd be forced to defend myself with my dad's pruning shears? I would find out just as soon as I crossed 56th Street.

Almost five hours later, I reached a cave high on the buttes' south side. Not only was I still unscathed, but I'd seen a flight of Mearn's quail, heard the cooing of mourning doves, and watched jackrabbits and roadrunners race through the brush. To top it off, I saw my first wily coyote. A startling contrast to life in Chicago.

I don't know how many times I made that expedition to the buttes, but each time I glimpsed a part of myself that stayed hidden in civilization.

These urban backyard day hikes, including Papago Park, are a place to start if you've never hiked in Arizona. This "neighborhood" taste of the wilds may save you from getting in over your head on longer, more strenuous treks. If hiked regularly, or used in combination with other aerobic exercise, these hikes give a convenient, reliable way to train for more challenging hikes.

Each hike is rewarding, giving urban Arizonans and visitors their own glimpse of the wild when they can't break away for a whole weekend. — *John Annerino*

Phoenix backyard hikes

Squaw Peak Park

With the possible exception of the Bright Angel Trail in the Grand Canyon, no other Arizona hiking trail is as popular as the 1.2-mile-long trail switchbacking its way to the 2,608-foot summit of Phoenix's Squaw Peak. According to rangers, roughly 500,000 people hike Squaw Peak every year. Even in midsummer heat, no fewer than 1,000 people per day make the hike, and on a spring weekend 3,000 people per day may be on the trail.

With those figures, you'd think that Squaw Peak was the only mountain in the state. Hardly. It is simply one of the most accessible and rewarding hikes in the Phoenix metropolitan area. Just remember to dress wisely and take lots of water. The heat can surprise you.

The trail climbs quickly through ocotillo, paloverde, creosote, and barrel and saguaro cactus. Fat, timid lizards called chuckwallas are a common sight. You may even see a black, yellow, and orange-beaded lizard called a Gila monster. The Gila woodpecker is as common on Squaw Peak as the coveys of mourning dove and Gambel's quail.

If you don't quite have the snap to make the pull all the way to the summit, there's a good turnaround point about three-quarters of a mile up the trail. It's at the foot of the last series of switchbacks and is marked by a paloverde tree shading an old mine shaft.

From the craggy summit you'll have an uninterrupted, 360-degree panorama of easily identifiable natural landmarks: The southern terminus of the Bradshaw Mountains can be seen to the north; Pinnacle Peak will be that lone finger of rock on the north end of the McDowell Mountains in the northeast; the main massif of the Superstition Mountains will be due east; South Mountain, shadowed by the sawteeth of the 4,000-foot-high Sierra Estrellas, will be south-southwest; and the White Tank Mountains will be almost due west. — *John Annerino*

- **How To Get There:** To reach the heart of Squaw Peak Park, and 1.2-mile Summit Trail, drive on Lincoln Drive or Glendale Avenue (they join at 16th Street) to Squaw Peak Drive, just west of 24th Street. Take Squaw Peak Drive to the first ramada on the left (north) side of the road and park there, space permitting. Summit Trail was designated a National Recreation Trail, so trailhead is marked.
- **Primary Access:** Squaw Peak Summit Trail via Squaw Peak Drive.
- **Elevation:** 1,400 feet at trailhead to 2,608 feet on summit. If you use Squaw Peak to train for hiking the Grand Canyon, as many do, build up gradually until you can hike up and down the summit four times in a day, two days in a row, with a pack on. That's your best indication of the stamina required to hike up and down the Bright Angel Trail.
- **Mileage:** 2.5 miles round trip.
- **Seasons:** Fall through spring; in summer, it's best to hike at dawn or dusk.

- **Maps:** USGS Sunnyslope quadrangle, or the Phoenix Mountain Trails Map.
- **Backcountry Information:** Permit not required. Fires and overnight camping prohibited. No dogs or mountain bikes on Summit Trail.

South Mountain Park

above: Vibrant brittlebush — silver leaves, golden daisy-like flowers — grow in a tumble, speared by more sedate saguaros, on a craggy Squaw Peak slope.
TOM DANIELSEN

Compared to the convenience and popularity of Squaw Peak, South Mountain can seem like a distant cousin. However, its 30 miles of main trails comprise a network that provides access to the largest municipal park in the world.

You can hike to the 2,330-foot summit ridge from the general vicinity of 24th Street south of Baseline Road via the 2-mile-long Mormon Trail, or from 7th Street south of Dobbins on the Holbert Trail. Or you can traverse the entire mountain via the 13.75-mile-long Sun Circle National Trail. You'll be traveling a mountain range long recognized by the Pima Indians as having spiritual significance. If you spend enough time out there studying the ancient petroglyphs, it will probably hold a similar significance for you.

One of the most popular hikes in South Mountain is the segment of the Sun Circle National Trail between Pima Canyon, on the eastern end of the park, west to

Buena Vista Lookout atop the summit ridge. This 3-mile-long segment of the National Trail meanders through Hidden Valley, where you'll be out of sight of metropolitan Phoenix and surrounded by desert wilderness. You'll briefly experience the land the way it was when the ancient Hohokam people roamed the area 2,000 years ago.

This is an enchanting journey through primeval shapes of decomposed granite, like the natural slickwalled slot called Fat Man's Pass, the rock tunnel, and the natural bridge. If you're attentive, you may be able to pick out an elephant tree or two. South Mountain is as far north as this unusual desert tree grows. — *John Annerino*

■ **How To Get There:** Reach the Sun Circle National Trail to Hidden Valley by driving south on Central Avenue to the park entrance (ask the park rangers for a free map) and continuing up the mountain to Buena Vista Lookout atop South Mountain. Take the trail east to Hidden Valley. Or, for the challenge of hiking uphill rather than downhill, take Guadalupe Road west into Pima Canyon on the eastern end of the mountain and begin your hike at the parking lot there. (To reach Guadalupe Road, take Interstate 10 to the Baseline Road exit, turn right, or west, on Baseline, then turn left, or south, on 48th Street, and drive south to Guadalupe Road.)

From either trailhead, you can do an out-and-back hike to Hidden Valley or car shuttle by parking a vehicle at each trailhead.

below: Shutting city noise away behind its rocky ridges, South Mountain Park offers sanctuary. Enjoy the Mexican gold poppies without fear, but the cholla cacti spreading their low spiky arms are to be avoided altogether.
GEORGE STOCKING

opposite page: Even when South Mountain looks baked and bleak, people still endure the summer sun to clamber Phoenix's mountain park trails past the rocks and the saguaros.
TOM DANIELSEN

- **Elevation:** 1,500 feet at Pima Canyon; 2,300 feet at Buena Vista Lookout.
- **Mileage:** Approximately 3 miles one way.
- **Seasons:** Fall through spring.
- **Maps:** USGS Lone Butte and Guadalupe quadrangles, or the Phoenix Mountain Trails map.
- **Backcountry Information:** Park rangers emphasize that all trails have rugged, rocky, and steep sections and that hikers need to carry water at all times. Call for information on city park regulations and on bike and horse trails.

Usery Mountain Park

above: A Pass Mountain vantage point looks toward the McDowell Mountains. JERRY SIEVE
opposite page: In spring, the Wind Cave Trail hobnobs with rowdy wildflowers — the magenta blooms of hedgehog cactus and the bright yellow flowers of brittlebush. JERRY SIEVE

Each time I reach this trail junction, I ask myself: Stay on Wind Cave Trail up Pass Mountain? Or hike the loop around the mountain's base?

My companion wanted a gentle hike and a sweeping view of metropolitan Phoenix. Wind Cave Trail, about 30 miles east of downtown Phoenix, certainly qualified. Two children skipped by us easily, their parents following, the mother toting an infant in a carrier slung on her back.

"Let's go that way," my companion said, pointing toward the disappearing kids.

So I left the 7.1-mile Pass Mountain Loop Trail for another day. It's longer, and, while over mostly flat or rolling terrain, it has steep inclines. Wind Cave Trail takes hikers gently but steadily up nearly 800 feet over a 1.6-mile stretch extending into the Tonto National Forest.

You won't find a real cave here, but take this hike in the Usery Mountains to view an array of Sonoran Desert vegetation; watch small mammals and perhaps a Gila monster putter about; and enjoy a sense of walking where desperados once roamed. The "cave," a recess cut by wind and water, reaches only a few feet into volcanic rock on Pass Mountain's western face.

Now, in late winter, the yellow of gold poppies and brittlebush stood out amid purple-black volcanic rocks. Bees hummed among the lupines. Peering over the slope with binoculars, we counted eight types of cacti: chain fruit, saguaro, buckhorn, teddy bear cholla, jumping cholla, barrel, hedgehog, and pincushion.

Bird-watchers can spot canyon towhees, mourning doves, woodpeckers, wrens, Gila woodpeckers. Come spring, hummingbirds would sip at chuparosa blooms.

Nearing Wind Cave, the trail became a bit steeper and harder to walk because of small, loose stones and an occasional step-up from one level to another.

From the "cave," our view stretched 40 or more miles to the south, west, and north; the 560-foot-high fountain at Fountain Hills seemed no bigger than a water gun's spurt.

Leaving my companion, I trekked the unmaintained trail to the top of Pass Mountain. After 20 minutes, with some bouldering, I reached the 3,312-foot summit, about 1,200 feet above the valley floor and with a grand 360-degree view of the Superstition, Mazatzal, and Usery mountains.

I rejoined my companion at the cave, and we hiked back down for a picnic lunch under a ramada in the recreation area. — *Robert Albano*

- **How To Get There:** Usery Mountain Recreation area is located 12 miles northeast from central Mesa. Take U.S. Route 60 east to Ellsworth/Usery Pass Road and go north 7.5 miles to the park turnoff on the right. You may also go east on McDowell or McKellips to Ellsworth/Usery Pass Road and go north 2 miles. At the park entrance, take Usery Park Road to Wind Cave Drive, turn left and park at road's end. The park is open 6 A.M. to 7 P.M. daily.
- **Elevation:** About 1,700 feet at the trailhead; 2,500 feet at the cave; and 3,312 feet at the summit.
- **Mileage:** 1.6 miles, one way, to the "cave".
- **Seasons:** Spring and fall are cooler; spring's wildflower season (February through March) is especially colorful.
- **Maps:** USGS Apache Junction quadrangle.
- **Attractions:** The 3,648-acre park has 50 picnic sites, 73 individual campsites, two reservation-only group campgrounds, an archery range, and a firearms shooting facility.

Papago Park

Papago Park is a major Phoenix destination, and not just for casual hikers. Its 1,200 acres hold well-equipped picnic sites; fishing lagoons; bike paths; the Phoenix Zoo; the Desert Botanical Garden; an archery range; and a golf course.

The park's Urban Wildlife Nature Trail is approximately .5 mile long and a relatively easy hike. Plants and wildlife are protected in the park, so enjoy a slice of desert life less than 1 mile off State Route 202. Other trails provide opportunities for hiking, horseback riding, and orienteering.

Papago Buttes, sometimes almost purple when the light's just right, easily catch the eye. The distinctive red rock (iron oxide-hematite) formed perhaps 6 to 15 million years ago. Pitted and pockmarked, the buttes were scarred when water broke up pockets of certain minerals, creating natural holes called tafoni. Be sure to look for the most outstanding tafoni, Hole-in-the-Rock, an eroded formation of arkosic conglomerate sandstone.

At Hole-in-the-Rock, a fissure lets a ray of sunlight trace positions on the floor throughout the year. The prehistoric people of the Sonoran Desert, the Hohokam, probably noticed this and used Hole-in-the-Rock to mark solstices and equinoxes.

To reach Papago Park from downtown Phoenix, take State 202 east to the

Priest Road/Center Parkway exit. Go north on Priest through the intersection with Van Buren Street, where Priest becomes Galvin Parkway. Continue north on Galvin to the stoplight at the Papago Park/Phoenix Zoo turnoff (less than .5 mile from the freeway exit). Turn right into the entrance drive, but keep curving left around the zoo's parking lot and into Papago Park.

Camelback Mountain/Echo Canyon

The most popular trail up Camelback Mountain leaves the east end of the Echo Canyon parking lot, which is located just south of the Tatum Boulevard/McDonald

Drive intersection. From the parking lot, head east uphill to the headwall, which forms the foundation for a spire of conglomerate rock called the Praying Monk. The Camelback Mountain Trail contours the base of this headwall east/southeast, until it gains a prominent ridgeline, which will take you all the way to Camelback's summit.

Don't underestimate this trail. It is steeper and longer than the Squaw Peak Summit Trail. It's not as well maintained, but it's not nearly as heavily used either. You need sturdier shoes for hiking this trail than you might get by with on Squaw Peak, and they should also have good traction. Several stretches on the upper section of trail require some boulder-dancing as well as walking on a natural ball bearing-type surface. For these reasons, this trail requires more care coming down than hiking up.

above: Squinting against the afternoon sun, this hiker takes in a golden view of the city from his perch atop Camelback Mountain.
EDWARD McCAIN

Camelback Mountain Trail is approximately 4 miles round trip. Allow plenty of time not only to hike it, but to marvel at the amazing rock formations and spectacular views of the Phoenix area.

White Tank Mountain Regional Park

The canyons in this Maricopa County mountain preserve have been scoured by generations of flash floods until natural catch basins, or tanks, formed in the exposed white granite. A network of trails range back into the White Tank Mountains and offer a generous selection of hikes.

You can enjoy a casual loop walk for less than 2 miles (like the 1.3-mile Black Rock Trail), take advantage of two short barrier-free trails, or stretch youself for a longer hike (say, the 8.8-mile round-trip hike to Ford Canyon). Connect to the Waterfall Trail if you want to relax with the unexpected — the trail leads to seasonal

above: They look silvery soft, haloed by the sun, but these teddy bear cholla in the White Tank Mountains should never be petted. Their "fuzz" is actually thousands of tiny gleaming cactus needles.
LES DAVID MANEVITZ

opposite page: Ancient symbols etched on stone, these curious Hohokam petroglyphs still puzzle us along Waterfall Trail in White Tank Mountain Regional Park.
LES DAVID MANEVITZ

pools and a sometimes-rushing waterfall. Mountain bikers, equestrians, family campers, backcountry campers — all can have fun in mountains that are just a matter of minutes on the interstate from downtown Phoenix.

Even though the park is on Phoenix's doorstep, it keeps its own ancient mystique; archaeologists have found Hohokam village sites and petroglyph panels (prehistoric drawings on rocks). Some trails may get rocky and rough in their upper reaches, but keep an eye out for your own petroglyph sighting.

Drive west of Phoenix on Interstate 10 to the Cotton Lane exit; go north 7 miles to Olive Avenue (Dunlap Avenue in Phoenix becomes Olive at 43rd Avenue). Then take Olive west for 15 miles to reach the park.

McDowell Mountain Regional Park

There are between 45 and 55 miles of well-maintained trails in McDowell Mountain Regional Park. Among them lies a portion of the historic military road

that was once the cavalry trail between Fort McDowell on the Indian reservation and Fort Whipple at the Territorial capital in Prescott. Nestled between the McDowell Mountains and the Verde River, this Maricopa County park displays the Sonoran Desert at its beautiful best, especially during the spring blooming time of mid-March to mid-April.

The mountain slopes have been forested with statuesque saguaros, but a 1995 lightning fire charred many acres. It's worth a fall afternoon jaunt just to see how the desert has coped with this trauma. Meander along a gentle nature trail, ride your horse or mountain bike, or see how far you can go on the Pemberton Trail; the Pemberton is a very challenging 15.3-mile loop. If you can't get enough in one day, don't fret, because there is a campground.

Located northeast of central Phoenix, McDowell Mountain Park is 4 miles north of Fountain Hills. From State Route 101 take Shea Boulevard east to Fountain Hills Boulevard; Fountain Hills Boulevard meanders northerly until it connects with McDowell Mountain Road near the park entrance.

above: As if calling up the sunrise, saguaro and cholla cacti look east from the McDowell Mountains into the Fort McDowell Indian Reservation. DAVID H. SMITH

Estrella Mountain Regional Park

Perhaps the name Sierra Estrella (Spanish for "Star Mountain") was imaginatively inspired by the white quartz outcroppings found throughout the length of the range.

You won't literally find fallen stars here, but there are approximately 50 miles of well-maintained trails to revel in at Estrella Mountain Regional Park, along with extensive recreation facilities (ball fields, rodeo arena). You can pick up a trail guide at the park for a day hike, or do a little primitive camping and hike again in the morning.

To reach the park, drive west of Phoenix on Interstate 10 to Estrella Parkway, Exit 126, then south 5 miles to the park entrance, which is just south of Indian Springs Road.

below: Scattered clouds offer fleeting shade over the Sierra Estrellas' ridges and foothills in Estrella Mountain Regional Park.
LES DAVID MANEVITZ

Superstition Wilderness

Just east of metropolitan Phoenix — a sprawling urban force on the desert floor — there are 35 named trails that lead into the legendarily secretive backcountry of the Superstition Wilderness. They run the gamut from primary trails to unmaintained trails.

A total of 12 trailheads provide access to these trails, with the Peralta and First Water trailheads being the most heavily used. (If you've hiked these two in the past, but it's been a while, be aware that the Forest Service now charges a daily use fee at both Peralta and First Water trailheads.) Plan your hike into this area based on your temperament, level of experience, and available time. Just remember, you've got about 150 miles of trail to explore in a wilderness that, so far, has kept its secrets.

Not that the Superstition Mountains don't entice the casual weekend hiker with moderate trails easily enjoyed in a day, but they don't especially look welcoming as they loom stark and imposing on the eastern horizon. In early days, they were the refuge of hermits, eccentrics, and gold seekers. Even today, behind their dark volcanic cliff faces — somewhere, treasure hunters still hope — might be the Lost Dutchman Mine. Just don't let gold fever distract you from taking your water, reading your map, and remembering your landmarks.

Fremont Saddle — Leaving from the Peralta Canyon trailhead for Fremont Saddle is one particular hike in the Superstition Mountains that gets a lot of traffic. Probably the most popular day hike in these mountains, the Peralta draws as many as 500 people through its trailhead on a busy spring day, and with good reason — the view from Fremont Saddle. On a clear spring morning, you'll think you could almost touch Weavers Needle.

When you reach that vista, stand there and ponder the words of Pedro de Castañeda, diarist for early Spanish explorers. He wrote in 1545: "Granted that they did not find the riches of which they had been told; they did find the next best thing — a place in which to search for them."

above: Against the cliffs of the Superstitions, the chain fruit cholla cactus hints that this is desert country. The rounded slopes, freshly green from February rains, gayly pretend otherwise with a display of Mexican goldpoppies.
TOM DANIELSEN

Going to Fremont Saddle is a moderate hike along a route that climbs 1,400 vertical feet in its 2.25-mile length. An excellent day's outing, fall through spring, it's most heavily hiked during colorful springtime, when the wildflowers are in bloom.

To reach the Peralta trailhead, take U.S. Route 60 east from Apache Junction, and go about 8.5 miles to the Peralta Road (Forest Service Road 77) turnoff on your left. Take FR 77 about 8 miles northeast to the Peralta Canyon trailhead.

Lost Dutchman State Park — This handy, lush park is another good launching point for comfortably venturing into the Superstitions. The area around the park contains some of the Sonoran Desert's more dramatic landscape. The 2.4-mile Treasure Loop Trail gradually climbs along the base of the Superstition Mountains. Two short trails, Jacobs Crosscut and Prospectors View, connect the Treasure Loop to Siphon Draw Trail. From Lost Dutchman's campground, Siphon Draw Trail follows a canyon about 3 miles to the top of the cliffs. Jacobs Crosscut is now a 7.5-mile hiking, horse, and bike trail. Trailheads are at the end of East Broadway Road, where it reaches the Tonto National Forest's boundary, and off of Firstwater Road, FR 78.

To reach Lost Dutchman State Park, take U.S. Route 60 east of Mesa to the Idaho Road exit, then go north on Idaho Road to University Drive/Superstition Boulevard in Apache Junction. From this junction, Idaho Road angles northeast and becomes State Route 88 (the Apache Trail). Go about 5 miles on State 88, and the park's entrance drive will be on your right.

To reach the Firstwater trailhead, leave the park and get back on State 88; turn right (northeast) and go .6 mile to the turnoff on your right. FR 78 will angle a little more easterly for about 2 miles until you reach the trailhead.

Open for overnight camping, Lost Dutchman State Park is convenient, but isolated enough from city lights to be a favored star-gazing spot. You'll be awed by how many stars you can suddenly see on a clear Arizona night. Maybe you'll camp on a night when there's a seasonal meteor shower — something you would have missed if you'd stayed in town.

Tucson Backyard Hikes

Sabino Canyon

The most popular hiking access point into the Santa Catalina Mountains is the Sabino Canyon Recreation Area. Since Sabino Canyon is not open to cars, that leaves three ways to visit this lush canyon: Take a guided shuttle from the visitor center up to road's end near the wilderness boundary and hike back down the paved Sabino Canyon Road; hike up the road to one of five streamside picnic areas and catch the shuttle back; or hike above Sabino Creek along the well-marked Phone Line Trail to the Sabino Creek junction 4.2 miles from the visitor center. (Shuttle tickets are sold next to the visitor center.)

At this junction, you can hike back the same way, stroll along the road paralleling the creek, or — if you're winded from the hike up — catch the shuttle back. — *John Annerino*

above: A scarf of fall color swaths the creek banks in Sabino Canyon.
DAVID W. LAZAROFF
opposite page: Giant saguaros rise green against the snow-tipped Santa Catalina Mountains.
DAVID W. LAZAROFF

- **How To Get There:** Take the Grant Road exit from Interstate 10 to Tanque Verde Road on the northeast side of town. Turn left on Tanque Verde Road and follow it to Sabino Canyon Road. Make another left onto Sabino Canyon Road. Approximately 4 miles later you will find the visitor center parking area. You will need to buy a parking pass to use the Sabino Canyon parking lot.
- **Elevation:** 2,800 feet, visitor center; 3,460 feet, north end of Sabino Canyon Road.
- **Mileage:** 4.2 miles one way.
- **Escape Route:** Via Phone Line Trail to visitor center or end, or the safest-looking descent line to Sabino Canyon Road.
- **Seasons:** Fall through spring; summer can be hot on Phone Line. Beware of dangerous runoff in Sabino Creek during storms.
- **Maps:** USGS Sabino Canyon quadrangle; Coronado National Forest map.
- **Nearest Supply Point:** Tucson.
- **Backcountry Information:** Permit not required. No camping. No dogs. No bikes on Wednesdays and Saturdays. Bikes allowed other days before 9:00 A.M. and after 5:00 P.M. Check with ranger for fire restrictions.

Hugh Norris Trail/Saguaro National Park West

The 20,738-acre Tucson Mountain Unit, established in 1961, contains the western section of Saguaro National Park, which also includes the 63,360-acre Rincon Mountain Unit established in March 1933. The units preserve incredible stands of saguaro cactus growing in this rich biotic community. The best way to visit this small desert wilderness and view these stately giants is to day hike up the Hugh Norris Trail in the Tucson Mountains.

The 5.5-mile-long Hugh Norris Trail is, for all practical purposes, a ridge trail. Its appeal lies not only in the airy views it offers while hiking most sections of it, but you actually get to the top of 4,687-foot-high Wasson Peak, where the 360-degree panorama is even better. To get there, you have to pay some minor dues in the form of switchbacks that begin about one-half mile after you leave the trailhead. The trail is well-marked and maintained its entire length.

Three miles out you'll come to the junction of the Sendero Esperanza Trail. This is a good cache point, or turnaround point if you're not feeling your oats. Wasson Peak is 2.5 miles beyond this junction, but you must first climb over the 4,500-foot-high saddle on the south side of Amole Peak before tackling the spiral of switchbacks that will take you up to the summit ridge of Wasson Peak.

From Wasson's summit, you can clearly see Baboquivari Peak to the southwest; Mount Wrightson to the southeast; the Rincon Mountains due east; the front range of the Catalinas, northeast; and Newman Peak, northwest — the best view on any day hike in the Tucson area.

- **How To Get There:** Drive west from Tucson on Speedway Boulevard until it turns into Kinney Road. Turn right on Kinney Road and drive to the Red Hills information center. The 6-mile-long Bajada Loop Drive is located 1.5 miles beyond; turn right onto the Bajada Loop Drive, and the Hugh Norris trailhead is located 1 mile farther.
- **Elevation:** 2,600 feet at trailhead to 4,687 feet on Wasson Peak.
- **Mileage:** 11 miles round trip.
- **Escape Route:** Via Hugh Norris or Kings Canyon trail.
- **Seasons:** Fall through spring; summer can be a very hot trek.
- **Maps:** USGS Avra quadrangle.
- **Nearest Supply Point:** Tucson.
- **Backcountry Information:** No camping is permitted in the Tucson Mountain Unit (Saguaro National Park West), so no permits are issued for overnight hiking. Camping is permitted in the Rincon Mountain Unit (East). Permits are issued at the visitor center. Permit not required for day hiking. Dogs and campfires are prohibited. Bikes on established roads only. Park is open daylight hours only.

Starr Pass

Sunrise in the desert is a delicate experience during the summer months. When I started my walk on the Starr Pass Trail in the Tucson Mountains, it was 4:30 in the morning.

The relatively flat trail extends only 1.5 miles, and it doesn't take long to walk. I didn't want to step on any rattlesnakes in the dark, and I wanted to be done with my hike before the sun rose too high and hot.

The trail begins on a little saddle above a hidden valley and descends gently into a spectacular landscape of giant saguaros, chollas, prickly pears, and barrel cacti. A wash just before the trailhead holds something unusual in the desert: cattails mixed with mesquite trees, and, often, some standing water from a Central Arizona Project reservoir off to the left behind some hills. Anyone sitting quietly there in the early morning might see coyotes and deer sipping from the pools.

The trail winds down a slight hill into an enormous bowl between several low peaks in the Tucson Mountains. Saguaros, jojoba, and creosote bushes fill the middle of the bowl. The steep incline of Gates Pass rises off to the right, and Cat Mountain, where a legendary figure called El Tejano supposedly hid a treasure years ago, sits off to the left.

At .6 of a mile from the trailhead, you'll come to a junction. Turn left. The junction sign says it's 1.1 miles to Starr Pass. A short distance away, the trail comes to a "T"; go right and in .6 of a mile you'll be in Starr Pass, looking west into the miles of green desert that cover Avra Valley.

Today the route through the pass remains a trail or dirt road, and there's no indication left that, in the last century, Starr Pass served as the main wagon route connecting the silver mines at Quijotoa, on the Tohono O'odham (Papago) Indian Reservation to the south and west, with the rail line at Tucson.

Starr Pass Trail offers a scenic and easy walk, much of it on a narrow dirt road, and it can be extended considerably where it connects to the David Yetman Trail. It is very popular with mountain bikers, but in most places the route is wide enough to accommodate both foot and bicycle traffic. — *Sam Negri*

■ **How To Get There:** Both the Starr and Yetman Pass trails are within Pima County's Tucson Mountain Park, adjacent to Saguaro National Park's West Unit. To get to the Starr Pass trailhead in Tucson Mountain Park, drive west off Interstate 10 onto St. Mary's Road. The name changes to Anklam Road as you cross Silverbell Road. Continue west on Anklam to Players Club Drive, which will be on your left (south) side of the street. The street winds through the Starr Pass housing development 1.1 miles until it reaches Starr Pass Boulevard. Turn left onto Starr Pass and then turn right almost immediately onto an unnamed dirt road. Drive west the length of a city block and turn right onto another wide dirt road that veers into a large parking area. If you don't have a high-clearance vehicle, park there and walk the last .5 mile to the trailhead. You can drive to the trailhead, but the road gets rough for passenger vehicles.

This is also the park's equestrian staging area. The trailhead parking lot has limited space, so get there early; parking outside designated areas will be ticketed. The hours are 7 A.M. to 10 P.M. If you park after hours or overnight at the trailhead, be sure you get the permit (fee) to do so.

New trailhead facilities and access are being planned. Check ahead for latest information from Pima County Natural Resources (see address below).

- **Elevation:** Approximately 2,700 to 3,000 feet.
- **Mileage:** 1.5 miles one way.
- **Seasons:** These trails are never more fragrant than on a summer morning. Plan your hike to end around 8 A.M.
- **Maps:** Park trail map (fee). Order from Pima County Natural Resources, Parks and Recreation, 5955 Camino de la Tierra, Tucson, AZ 85741.
- **Nearest Supply Point:** Tucson.
- **Backcountry Information:** A word of caution. There is at least one abandoned mine shaft just off the trail. The mine is unfenced and dangerous. Avoid it.

Bear Canyon Trail/Seven Falls

For the shorter route, from the Sabino Canyon visitor center take the shuttle train to the lower Bear Canyon picnic area and Bear Canyon trailhead. Seven Falls is one of the prettiest waterfalls in southern Arizona. The hike up Bear Canyon is 2.2 miles one way. Be sure to wear comfortable shoes that you don't mind getting wet, because of the rocky, uneven trail and because you'll cross the creek many times.

For a longer trip, a choice 11-mile loop hike goes up Sabino Canyon and down Bear Canyon. Start at the visitor center and take the shuttle up Sabino Canyon to the end of the road. Hike 2.5 miles up the canyon, a well-marked trail, to Sabino Basin. The trail that crosses the ridge to the east into Bear Canyon is 2.1 miles long. From there on it's 4.3 miles to Seven Falls and another 2.2 miles back to the picnic area and the shuttle to your car.

opposite page: Bear Canyon Trail rewards sturdy hikers with views of Seven Falls, where a seasonal creek spills over tiered stony ledges. JACK DYKINGA

Tanque Verde Ridge/Saguaro National Park East

The 63,360-acre Rincon Mountain Unit composes the eastern section of Saguaro National Park; it also serves as park headquarters. From downtown Tucson take Broadway Boulevard east about 9 miles to Old Spanish Trail. Turn right (south) and go about 4.5 miles to the park entrance. Before you charge up Tanque Verde Ridge, stop in the visitor center for a brief orientation, then take Cactus Forest Drive 1 mile to the Javelina picnic area. The trailhead is off to the right (south).

If you're just interested in an hour's stroll, the mile-long hike up to an unnamed peak at 3,574 feet is as good a view of Tucson as you will get without climbing all the way up to 7,000-foot Tanque Verde Ridge. From Peak 3574, this well-marked trail begins climbing in earnest, 500 vertical feet per mile in

the 5 miles to the Juniper Basin campsite area. You can turn around at any point, but if you hike all the way to Juniper Basin, you will have some magnificent views of the saguaro forest and the Tucson Basin below and of 8,482-foot Rincon Peak above.

Catalina State Park

Located just off State Route 77, about 10 miles north of Tucson in the Santa Catalina foothills, Catalina State Park contains a nice variety of well-marked hiking trails. But what makes Catalina State Park hikes different are the spectacular views of the sheer rock cliffs of Pusch Ridge. As with Tucson's other backyard hikes, the best time of year is fall through spring, although dawn and late afternoon are delightful in summer. The park offers picnicking, camping, birding, and horseback riding, as well as easy trails (one goes to a Hohokam village site) and alluring day hikes. Some canyon streams form small, seasonal waterfalls and natural pools.

above: A brief drive from Tucson city streets, Catalina State Parks grants a gateway to retreats like these grasslands near Romero Canyon. GURINDER P. SINGH **opposite page:** The forest atop Mount Lemmon looks worlds away from the desert below. No saguaros and brittlebush, you'll find pines and the yellow flowers of sneezeweed. EDWARD McCAIN

Mount Lemmon Trail

An easy drive from downtown Tucson, the Mount Lemmon Trail skirts the top of the Santa Catalina Mountains at 9,157 feet, meanders through ponderosa pine forest, and crosses beautiful grassy meadows. In summer and early fall, sunflower and Indian paint brush decorate the mountainside. Even in the middle of summer, when Tucson's temperature soars to more than 100 degrees, this is a refreshingly cool place to hike.

From Tanque Verde Road in Tucson, take the Mount Lemmon Highway 30 miles to the top. The road's last mile, just past the ski lift, is especially steep and narrow. The trailhead is very close to a fenced compound of telescopes and communication towers. A Mount Lemmon topographic map, or the Pusch Ridge Wilderness map of the Santa Catalina Mountains, shows various trail options.

below: A view north from the Reef of Rocks on Mount Lemmon is just a sliver of the wild expanse beckoning the adventurous into the Santa Catalina Mountains.
PETER NOEBELS

Prescott Backyard Hikes

Thumb Butte Trail

It is a toss-up when you try to decide which is the most popular hiking trail in the Prescott National Forest — the Thumb Butte Trail #33 or Granite Mountain Trail. A 1.5-mile loop, the Thumb Butte Trail is certainly the shorter and easier of the two. It makes one of the best introductory hikes to the area before you tackle one of the longer, steeper, and less-accessible summits.

This well-maintained trail climbs about 600 feet in the first mile to the main saddle on the southwest ridge of Thumb Butte. A half-mile up this trail, you will see the remains of a rough-hewn, one-room log cabin. It is characteristic of those once used by gold seekers who prospected near Miller Creek and dug "glory holes" elsewhere in the Bradshaw Mountains during the 1800s. Placards posted along this enchanting trail identify local flora such as Gambel oak, manzanita, and agave.

From Thumb Butte saddle, you can picnic or nap under a nearby alligator juniper before heading back the way you came. Or, if you're an experienced hiker, you can tackle the summit of Thumb Butte. To reach the actual summit, you need to negotiate loose boulders to follow a rough secondary trail northeast from the saddle several hundred yards to the foot of the easiest-looking rock gully. Several unexposed boulder moves will take you up to the fluted summit of Thumb Butte.

From either the summit of Thumb Butte or its saddle, you'll be able to see monolithic Granite Mountain almost due north; the standing wave of the 7,000-foot-high Sierra Prieta rim immediately to your west; and 7,696-foot Spruce Mountain and neighboring Mount Union in the maze of green peaks to the southeast.

You can return to the trailhead and picnic area by the same route, or you can complete a loop hike by descending a shorter and steeper, well-marked and paved trail that switchbacks off the northwest side of Thumb Butte.

- **How To Get There:** Drive west through Prescott on Gurley Street until it turns into the Thumb Butte Road, then drive 3 miles farther to the Thumb Butte picnic area and trailhead. The 6,514-foot-high volcanic landmark will be off to your left; a large sign highlighting the Thumb Butte trail system marks the trailhead.
- **Primary Access:** Thumb Butte picnic area.
- **Elevation:** Approximately 5,700 feet at the trailhead to 6,514 feet on the summit.
- **Mileage:** 1.5-mile loop.
- **Seasons:** Spring through fall is most popular.
- **Maps:** USGS Iron Springs quadrangle and Prescott National Forest recreation map.
- **Nearest Supply Point:** Prescott.
- **Backcountry Information:** No permit required.

Granite Mountain Wilderness

Only a couple of areas in Arizona share the peculiar characteristics of the 9,800-acre Granite Mountain Wilderness: Cochise Stronghold in the Dragoons of southeastern Arizona and Hualapai Mountain County Park in the northwest. They all look more like islands of exposed stone than mountains.

In the case of 7,626-foot-high Granite Mountain, nearly 50 percent of the wilderness is exposed granite. Rock climbers come from all over the Southwest to climb its immaculate-looking, 500-foot-high, south-facing buttress. It also makes for some exceptional hiking, if you stick to its main trails.

Trail 261 is known locally as the Granite Mountain Trail, and it is the main access into Granite Mountain Wilderness. Go west from the trailhead gate a little more than 1 mile to Blair Pass, the junction at Trail 37 and 261. The trail to the right is Trail 261. Walk through the wooden chute and hike about 1.5 miles of moderate switchbacks to Granite Mountain Saddle. If you keep your eyes open en route, you may see rock climbers on the mountain's main buttes. You can turn back at the saddle, or you can continue hiking another mile through the ponderosas to Granite Mountain Overlook.

Looking south from the overlook, you'll see 7,089-foot Little Granite Mountain immediately in front of you, a small finger of granite called Lizard Head a bit to the southeast, and Thumb Butte rearing its gnarly head at the foot of the Sierra Prietas.

The summit area of Granite Mountain is sheltered by huge granite boulders and tenacious-looking ponderosas. It is an ideal place to camp if you're not troubled by the fact that you'll be sleeping in prime mountain lion habitat. This is one of the densest concentrations of that magnificent animal in the state. They like rocks, too.

above: Hikers pass some of the many granite boulders along the trail climbing Granite Mountain.
GEORGE H.H. HUEY

- ■ **How To Get There:** Hiking Trail 261 up to the Granite Mountain Saddle, or to its summit, makes for an exhilarating day's outing for walkers and hikers of all ages. To reach the trailhead, take the Iron Springs Road 3 miles west from Prescott to the Granite Basin Lake turnoff. This is Forest Service Road 374, where you'll turn right and drive (or pedal) 5 miles to Trail 261.
- ■ **Primary Access:** Granite Mountain trailhead.
- ■ **Elevation:** 5,600 feet at trailhead to 7,626 feet on summit.
- ■ **Mileage:** 7 miles round trip.
- ■ **Seasons:** Spring through fall is the best time.

- **Maps:** USGS Iron Springs and Jerome Canyon quadrangles and Prescott National Forest recreation map.
- **Nearest Supply Point:** Prescott.
- **Backcountry Information:** No permit required. Use existing fire rings and dead and down wood. Beware of fire danger.

Spruce Mountain/Groom Creek Loop

Both main loop trails up Spruce Mountain provide excellent forest hikes, but the trees are actually Douglas and white firs amid tall ponderosa pines, with nary a spruce tree in sight. The Groom Creek loop on the west slope of Spruce Mountain is a moderate forest hike of 9 miles to the mountain's summit. The trail elevation starts at about 6,400 feet and goes to 7,600 feet. Allow about six hours to hike the loop.

Begin the Groom Creek Loop at the parking lot across FR 52 from the Horse Camp. Head north (left) on Trail 307, and it's a 2.8-mile brisk climb to the Forest Service lookout tower at the summit. Go south on the loop, and it's a 5.4-mile ramble along South Spruce Ridge to the top. Either direction, the trail is well marked all the way, and the nearly 9-mile loop makes for a good day's hike.

If your heart is not set on hiking all the way to the summit, you can cut nearly 2 miles off the trip by taking the unnumbered connector trail at Mile 1.5 on the north loop and connecting with the south loop on South Spruce Ridge at Mile 4.2.

The panoramic view from the summit includes Prescott, Prescott Valley, and the Bradshaw and Sierra Prieta ranges. The loop is a year-round trail, but some years, deep winter snows can close the trail to the top.

In Prescott, from the intersection of Gurley and Mount Vernon streets, drive south 6.5 miles on Mount Vernon which becomes the Senator Highway/Forest Service Road 52 to the trailhead parking lot across from the Groom Creek Horse Camp. To reach the summit trailhead, drive 4.5 miles south of Prescott on the Senator Highway and turn left at FR 52A. Drive another 4 miles to the fire tower picnic area parking lot.

West Spruce Mountain

Not to be confused with Spruce Mountain, West Spruce Mountain is approximately 5 miles west of Thumb Butte, via Forest Service Road 373, to the trailhead.

The trail, which follows the crest of the Sierra Prieta Range, is about 2.5 miles one way to West Spruce Mountain's summit at about 7,100 feet. The spectacular views en route overlook Copper Basin, so named in 1864 for the copper claims within it, and Skull Valley, said to be named for the piles of bleached Indian skulls found by the first white man who entered the area.

Flagstaff & Sedona Backyard Hikes

Inner Basin Trail/Flagstaff

Few hiking trails offer as much variety as the Inner Basin Trail near Flagstaff. Hikers, mountain bikers, cross-country skiers, amateur geologists, regional history buffs and flora-and-fauna watchers all flock to this very popular 2- to 3-mile trail. During spring and summer, wildflowers bloom along roads and trails leading into the San Francisco Peaks' interior valley, or Inner Basin. During the fall, aspen tree groves turn golden. And in wintertime, when snow lies heavy across roads and trails, cross-country skiers climb into the Inner Basin to enjoy a ski season that sometimes lasts until mid-June.

The length of a hike on the Inner Basin Trail depends on how far past the basin one ventures. Although it's somewhat steep, the ascent feels only moderately strenuous if you pace yourself. The trail starts in Lockett Meadow at the end of an unpaved road. Following a primitive rock-strewn roadbed — an ankle-twister for the unwary — the path climbs 1,100 feet through a ponderosa pine and aspen forest.

Ravens, Abert's squirrels, and Steller's jays sound their alarms from tree-branch lookouts. Elk and wild turkeys live deep in these woods, and in fall when berries ripen, you may encounter a black bear fattening itself for hibernation on juicy kinnikinnicks.

After 1.5 miles, the Inner Basin Trail comes to a junction at Jack Smith Spring, where water flows from an untreated tap. Historically, water has been scarce in Flagstaff, and beginning in the 1950s, wells that now supply the city were drilled throughout the Inner Basin. A few cabins clustered near Jack Smith Spring protect equipment used to pump and transport water off the mountain. The largest cabin serves as a winter shelter for federal and state snow surveyors who compute the watershed's spring runoff, which in turn predicts the region's water supply.

Continuing past Jack Smith Spring for another half-mile, the trail enters the Inner Basin. A quiet approach by hikers arriving near dawn or dusk may surprise elk grazing among succulent meadow grasses and forbs.

The cataclysmic forces that shaped the San Francisco Peaks appear quite evident within the Inner Basin's volcanic caldera, formed by glaciers into a broad U-shaped valley. Students of geology will note this unique carving effect of moving ice as well as the variously sized rocks and boulders scattered upon the valley floor by the melting glacier. Contrastingly, valleys formed by water look more V-shaped, and the rocks and boulders look as if they've been sorted according to size.

From the meadow, at approximately 10,000 feet, you can trace the remnants of old lava flows. And, although heavy aspen forests cover most inclines, cleared tracks on high-peak talus slopes show where powerful avalanches leveled everything in their paths.

The trail offers something for everyone — geology buffs, birders, wildlife watchers, leaf peepers, and just plain old outdoor enthusiasts. — *Tom Dollar*

opposite page:
Alpine meadows like the Inner Basin's offer watchful visitors a chance to spot elk and bear.
GEORGE STOCKING

- **How To Get There:** In the Kachina Peaks Wilderness about 146 miles north of Phoenix; about 15 miles north of Flagstaff. From Flagstaff, drive north on U.S. Route 89 for 12.5 miles to Forest Service Road 552, which is .8 of a mile past the turnoff to Sunset Crater Volcano National Monument. Turn left (west) onto FR 552 and continue for approximately 1 mile to the Lockett Meadow sign. Turn right (north), and drive 3 miles to the trailhead. The dirt road to Lockett Meadow is narrow and winding. A high-clearance vehicle is recommended. Snowdrifts may block the road in early spring and late fall.
- **Elevation:** 8,800 feet to 10,200 feet.
- **Mileage:** 2 miles to Lockett Meadow.
- **Seasons:** May (late spring) through October.
- **Maps:** USGS Humphreys Peak quadrangle; Coconino National Forest map.
- **Nearest Supply Point:** Flagstaff.
- **Backcountry Information:** This is a hiking trail only — no mountain bikes are allowed because no mechanized or motorized vehicles, including bicycles, can be used in official wilderness areas. There is no camping in the Inner Basin in order to protect the watershed. Above the tree line, there is no camping and no off-trail hiking. Always check with the ranger district about fire restrictions.

Brins Mesa Trail/Sedona

The Brins Mesa Trail begins mere blocks from Uptown Sedona, climbing 1.5 miles to a tabletop aerie sandwiched between Brins Ridge and Wilson Mountain. The highlight of this hike is the view, and Sedona's red rock landmarks play starring roles. The 1-mile point — where the real climb begins — offers an ideal turnaround for novices, while the strong of lung might take on the steep half mile to the mesa's edge.

The trail, which begins at the gate to the old shooting range, winds through fresh-scented cypress and piñon. Manzanita bushes line the route; their entwined maroon-and-silver branches hang with delicate pink-and-white bells in spring, becoming tiny rust-colored "apples" by fall. Despite the lush vegetation, the wide trail conveys an open feeling.

Dominating to the north and east are Shiprock, with its triangular "sail" of cream-colored Coconino sandstone; Steamboat, whose "smokestacks" tower above a sandstone prow of reddish orange; and the long ridge called The Fin. As the trail meanders toward the mesa (a flat expanse sloping up to the north), the Cibola Mitten and Brins Ridge guard the western flank.

At a low spot, about three-quarters of a mile along, the trail forks. The left fork continues the climb to Brins Mesa, named in memory of a wily brindle-colored bull that evaded roundup on the mesa's high pastures. As the story goes, a pair of cowboys finally roped Old Brin, but he dragged them into the brush. Rather than continue the struggle, they shot him.

After about 25 minutes at a good clip, hikers reach a series of natural red rock steps leading up to a broad bench in the Schnebly Hill formation, a perfect spot to

pause, catch their breath, and identify more of Sedona's "rock stars."

Snoopy and Camel Head overlook Uptown Sedona and sycamore tree-studded Oak Creek Canyon. Farther south loom the mirror-image Twin Buttes. Sharp-eyed hikers may spot Gibraltar, Courthouse, and Bell Rock peeking out from behind them. To the southeast rises Mitten Ridge, incorporating Giant's Thumb and Teapot Rock.

Closer, at the base of the highest peak in Sedona — 7,122-foot basalt-crowned Wilson Mountain — stand several red rock spires. One of the largest, Earth Angel, appears with wings folded and hands in a prayerful position.

Those who want a short hike should turn around here. For others, who share Old Brin's love of heights and open spaces, the rocky trail ascends steeply but rewards with stunning views in every direction. The grassy mesa spreads out and invites exploration, a pleasant surprise after the hard climb. From there I once watched a misty ephemeral waterfall dancing in the wind, a rare but stirring sight created by spring melt plunging from high on Wilson Mountain.

With a good map and a car shuttle, experienced hikers can plan variations with connecting trails or simply return to the original trailhead. — *Kathleen Bryant*

- **How To Get There:** From Uptown Sedona, take Jordan Road north; turn left onto West Park Ridge Drive, which ends at a dirt parking area. A sign indicates Brins Mesa No. 119.

  Parking on Coconino National Forest land here requires a Red Rock Pass, sold at four visitor centers in the Sedona vicinity (see Chapter 7). Stay on the trail and be respectful of nearby private property.

- **Elevation:** 4,200 to 4,600 feet.
- **Mileage:** 3 miles one way.
- **Seasons:** All year, although spring and fall feel most comfortable; summer can be hot.
- **Maps:** USGS Munds Park, Wilson Mountain quadrangles; Coconino National Forest map.
- **Nearest Supply Point:** Sedona.
- **Backcountry Information:** This trail crosses the Red Rock/Secret Mountain Wilderness; official wilderness areas do not allow bicycle use (or any other mechanized or motorized travel). Please do not disturb ruins or artifacts.

A.B. Young Trail/Sedona

Sitting on a flat boulder perched on the rim, I see tiny cars winding up the road between Sedona and Flagstaff in Oak Creek Canyon.

Two hours ago, I started up the A.B. Young Trail on the west side of Oak Creek, a literal hop-skip-and-a-jump on stepping-stones crossing the creek from Bootlegger Campground. Sometimes called the East Pocket Trail, the route begins in ponderosa pine and oak as it climbs abruptly away from the creek into the Red Rock/Secret Mountain Wilderness.

Going up, the pines gave way to low-growing manzanita, mountain mahogany, and scrub oak. The trail became a series of switchbacks, exposing the splendors of Oak Creek Canyon.

Once a livestock trail in the late 1800s, today the trail is in excellent shape, smooth and gently graded, a bit cobbly only where it crosses rockslide debris.

Once on top, I followed the trail along the rim. Where the trail became indistinct, faint blaze marks and rock cairns led me west to the East Pocket Lookout, one of the state's last wooden fire-lookout towers.

Hike this route in spring and fall. To reach the A.B. Young Trail from Bootlegger Campground, a few miles north of Slide Rock State Park in Oak Creek Canyon, cross the creek opposite the middle of the campground and walk downstream a short way to a marked trailhead. Don't cross the stream in high water. Pay a fee to park in the campground. — *Tom Dollar*

Bell Rock Trail/Sedona

To reach the trailhead from the junction of State Route 89A and State 179 in Sedona, go south 6.5 miles on State 179. Park on the east side of the highway just south of Bell Rock. The 4-mile-long trail circles both Bell Rock and Courthouse Butte. The red rocks that make up the sculptural perfection of Bell Rock and Courthouse Butte were laid as beach sand maybe 280 million years ago in the flood-plain of a great river. The fine-grained rock has eroded into soul-stirring cliffs, buttes, and monuments.

Use Bell Rock and Courthouse Butte as landmarks because the route completely encircles the two unmistakable

below: The Bell Rock Trail winds through the high desert surrounding Courthouse Butte.
BOB AND SUZANNE CLEMENZ

rock formations. Several branches of the trail veer off in various directions, but the main trail is well-traveled and easy to locate. For the first few miles, it follows a nearly level contour along the north side of Bell Rock, across the short space to Courthouse Butte, and then on around the far end of Courthouse.

The easy trail with only a 250-foot elevation gain offers sweeping views of both Courthouse Butte and Bell Rock to the south and the rest of Sedona to the north.

On the back side of Courthouse Butte, the trail enters the Munds Mountain Wilderness (no bicycles allowed and all dogs must be leashed), climbing to near the top of Bell Rock at trail's end. The hike should take about two hours. Be sure to take water.

You can find the route on the 7.5-minute Sedona and the 7.5-minute Munds Mountain USGS topographic maps. — *Peter Aleshire*

above: Two hikers on the Kachina Trail savor a crisp afternoon, high above Flagstaff.
DAVID H. SMITH

Kachina Trail/Flagstaff

One October morning, my husband, Michael, and I heard an elk's frenzied bugling coming from a grove of aspens along the Kachina Trail. We spied movement among the trees, and Michael spotted the big-racked male and his harem of nearly 20 females.

A few lingering lupines reflected the blue of the cloudless sky. There was no better place to be that day than high on the San Francisco Peaks near Flagstaff.

The trail rambles through the Kachina Peaks Wilderness, a cool, moist forest of spruce, fir, and pine nestled amid lichen-splattered boulders. The open meadows along the way afford eye-popping views of Arizona's highest mountains.

Squirrels and jays chirred and chittered. A rumpled porcupine scrambled up a small fir tree to hide in the branches. Three mule deer snapped twigs as they turned tail and fled. A sapsucker flew to an aspen branch. A black bear had marked its passage by clawing away a tree's tender white bark.

This hike works well if you use two vehicles for shuttling and hike just one way. To reach the Kachina Trail, travel 7 miles north of Flagstaff on U.S. Route 180. Turn right onto Snow Bowl Road and drive 7 miles to the top. Turn right into the first parking lot, and the well-marked trailhead is at the lot's south end. For a one-way hike, travel up Snow Bowl Road 2.3 miles and turn right onto Freidlein Prairie Road, Forest Service Road 522. Bear left, go 4 miles to the end, and leave one vehicle here. In your second car, return to Snow Bowl Road and continue up to the main trailhead. This will allow a moderate hike of almost 6 miles, mostly downhill. — *Rose Houk*

Lockett Meadow/Flagstaff

above: Looking across Lockett Meadow in the fall, you can see aspens gilding the Inner Basin's slopes and October snows already dusting the San Francisco Peaks. ROBERT G. McDONALD
opposite page: The Kachina Trail meanders below the San Francisco Peaks among aspens in luminous fall display. DAVID H. SMITH

At 8,000 feet in the San Francisco Peaks, Lockett Meadow provides cathedral-like groves of aspen mingled with pine, spruce, and fir. Surrounded by the high San Francisco Peaks, this is a fabulous place to catch the rich fall color of aspens. There is good access to casual hiking along old dirt roads. The Peaks tend to make their own weather, and snow often arrives early.

To reach Lockett Meadow, take U.S. Route 89 north from Flagstaff. About .75 mile north of the Sunset Crater Volcano National Monument turnoff, turn west off U.S. 89 onto a Coconino National Forest Service Road. Just past a cinder mine, the gravelly road turns right and climbs steeply around Sugarloaf Mountain and, in 4 to 5 miles, reaches Lockett Meadow.

Long Canyon Trail/Sedona

I'm in Long Canyon, a sanctuary of melting snow and silver-green cypress trees, one of the wildest places near Sedona. As the raven flies, this is only 4 miles from Uptown Sedona's souvenir shops and tour buses, yet I am a world away from the heat and bustle.

I've passed only a few hikers as the 3-mile trail meanders up and down gentle knolls and across shallow washes tinkling with snowmelt. I usually hike Long Canyon in summer, when oak and maple leaves play peekaboo with the views. Today bare branches reveal towering Maroon Mountain and the reddish sandstone spires clustered below.

The sharp perfume of crushed pine needles rises from the forest floor to mingle with the musty scent of decaying leaves. Early-blooming drabas and lupines dot the undergrowth with yellow and lavender, and running or dripping water sounds a different note at almost every turn.

As the trail climbs, and I enter the heart of the box canyon, the vegetation changes from waist-high chaparral to dense forest. At about 2 miles, I leave the trail to rest on top of a large boulder and scan the cliffs for signs of the Sinagua people, who sheltered in alcoves here centuries ago.

above: Locals consider the hike through Long Canyon one of the best for viewing Sedona's red rock formations.
LARRY LINDAHL

Poison ivy often discourages me from exploring farther here, but today I continue through snow, not an itchy weed in sight. I follow the trail to the 3-mile point, where it ends at a steep bluff of sandstone. You may spot a few Indian ruins and rock pictographs; please enjoy them from a distance and don't disturb.

The Long Canyon trailhead is 6 miles northwest of Sedona. Take U.S. 89A to Dry Creek Road. Turn right, drive 2.5 miles to a T intersection. Turn right onto Long Canyon Road (FR 152D) and drive .5 mile to a parking area on the left, where a sign indicates Trail 122. The first 1.5 miles is exposed and hot in summer. — *Kathleen Bryant*

Marg's Draw Trail/Sedona

Sedona's Marg's Draw, despite its docile personality, takes you into a federally designated Wilderness with views of Sedona's red rock country that are hard to beat even on much more demanding hikes.

I set out in midafternoon on a short December day. Just beyond the trailhead, a gate marked the boundary of the Munds Mountain Wilderness. I marveled at such a wild place so close to town.

After a short climb, the trail leveled onto a flat, and there the views began. I headed into a bowl surrounded by fantastic red-rock cliffs. The faces of Munds Mountain, Lee Mountain, and the Crimson Cliffs peered through the previous night's snow.

The trail headed east toward Munds Mountain to a "T" intersection with a north-south trail. I took the right branch, winding south across the twin drainages of Marg's Draw. Had I turned left, the longer north fork would have led me to the Crimson Cliffs. At their base, the trail again divided, the left route circling to another trailhead on Schnebly Hill Road. the right fork switchbacked up the cliff to the erosional formation known as Snoopy Rock. If you use your imagination, the trail ends on Snoopy's foot.

On the southbound trail, I turned at the Broken Arrow parking area. In the later afternoon chill, it was empty.

Marg's Draw is easily reached from a trailhead at the end of Sombart Lane, off State Route 179 about .4 of a mile south of the Sedona "Y" intersection. Both the trailhead, accessible to the public through an agreement between the property owner and the City of Sedona, and the trail itself were extensively rebuilt in the 1990s. A map at the trailhead describes the routes, which cover about 3 miles total. Alternate access to the Marg's Draw Trail is on Schnebly Hill Road and the Broken Arrow parking area off Morgan Road. Like all designated Wilderness areas, Marg's Draw is open to foot and horse traffic, but closed to mechanized travel, including bicycles. — *Norm Tessman*

below: A hiker enjoys a wintertime vista from the trail at Marg's Draw.
MOREY K. MILBRADT

Mount Elden Trail/Flagstaff

Mount Elden's steep, well-worn trail to the 9,299-foot summit and a Forest Service lookout tower begins at a large parking lot at the wooded edge of the city within walking distance of fast-food restaurants.

Despite its accessibility, this is a steady huff-and-puff grind for 3 twisting uphill miles through a mix of pines, junipers, and bayonet cacti. And in May, when I climbed, remnants of snowpack slowed the way.

My hike up took more than two hours, but I dallied, talking to people and trying to focus binoculars while gulping thin air. Mount Elden affords expansive views to the horizons.

The Elden trail finally arrives on a narrow plateau that provides a view of the rugged heights of the San Francisco Peaks and the Kachina Peaks Wilderness, created when the dormant volcano blew out millennia ago, evaporating half a mountain.

The scars of a forest fire more than 30 years ago remain. The fire burned over the mountain and into the basin, leaving behind a moonscape, but new life gradually returns.

I watched three colorful hang gliders hover on the thermals overhead. Turkey Park, just below the summit, is a popular glider port reached by a dirt road from the basin.

In marked contrast to my climb up Elden, the descent dropped quickly back to Fatman's Loop, a flatland leisure trail that forms the lower Elden trail where it begins immediately east of the Peaks Forest Service office on U.S. 89 (Santa Fe Avenue) in east Flagstaff. For those who can't handle the strenuous nature of this hike, drive U.S. 180 about 2 miles north of Flagstaff to Schultz Pass Road (Forest Service Road 420). Turn right and follow it north, then east less than 1 mile to FR 557, which will take you to Elden's summit.

Carry water. There's none beyond the trailhead. Winter snow can close the upper Elden trail and the road. — *Tom Kuhn*

Observatory Mesa Trail/Flagstaff

I had walked maybe 200 yards up Observatory Mesa Trail, part of the Flagstaff Urban Trail System, when I spotted a small metal sign on an enormous ponderosa pine snag, a standing dead tree. "Wildlife tree," it read. "Saved for their food and shelter. Help to protect it."

Soaring more than 100 feet, the ponderosa was pocked with cavities bored by woodpeckers and flickers. Descending headfirst along the trunk, a busy pygmy nuthatch scoured the bark for bugs.

Observatory Mesa Trail, one of my favorite Flagstaff morning walks, begins amid a ponderosa pine woodland in Thorpe Park, just a few blocks from downtown. The noise of diesel locomotives rumbling along tracks through the city's center and of traffic humming along nearby highways is a constant on this hike, but don't let that throw you off. The trail provides a heart-pumping uphill walk, rising some 440 feet in just 1.6 miles. You can hike year-round, except when snow buries the pathway.

You'll likely have the company of other hikers and passing mountain bikers, sometimes trailed by their dogs.

At first, the trail winds through a ravine spilling off the mesa. After a half mile, it turns sharply left to climb the ridge. There it rises through the Lowell Observatory property, leveling off atop a mesa for an easy amble to the gate at trail's end. You can turn around and return to the trailhead or hike further along national forest jeep roads.

To reach the trailhead in Thorpe Park, take Santa Fe Avenue to Toltec and turn north to Thorpe Road. — *Tom Dollar*

Walnut Canyon National Monument/Flagstaff

Take 240 stairsteps down the hillside and amble along the paved Island Trail (.75 mile long) to more than a dozen prehistoric cliff dwellings in Walnut Canyon. At 7,000 feet elevation, this beautiful canyon has a mixture of vegetation from prickly pear cactus to stands of Douglas fir. This is an interesting one-hour walk, open year-round. Just remember that you'll be climbing *up* those 240 steps going back.

Walnut Canyon is 4 miles east of Flagstaff on Interstate 40, then go 3 miles south on an access road to the park entrance.

below: A visitor stops along the Island Trail to contemplate Sinagua daily life in this cliff dwelling at Walnut Canyon National Monument.
TOM BEAN

When You Go

Phoenix Backyard Hikes

**Squaw Peak Park, Papago Park,
South Mountain Park, and
Camelback Mountain**
www.ci.phoenix.az.us/PARKS/mntparks.html
Phoenix Parks, Recreation and Library
Department, (602) 262-6862;
TDD, (602) 262-6713.

Echo Canyon Recreation Area
at Camelback Mountain
(602) 256-3220

Papago Park
(602) 262-4837

South Mountain Park
(602) 495-0222

Squaw Peak Park
(602) 262-7901
(602) 262-6713 — TDD

**White Tank Mountain Regional
Park, McDowell Mountain Regional Park,
Estrella Mountain Regional Park, and
Usery Mountain Recreation Area**
www.maricopa.gov/rec_svc
Maricopa County Parks and Recreation
Department, (602) 506-2930.

White Tank Mountain Regional Park
(623) 935-2505
Entry fee, overnight permits.
Call about camping fees, backcountry
restrictions. Open 6 A.M. to 8 P.M., Sunday
through Thursday; 6 A.M. to 10 P.M., Friday
and Saturday.

McDowell Mountain Regional Park
(480) 471-0173
Entry fee.
Call for camping fees.

Estrella Mountain Regional Park
(623) 932-3811
Entry fee.
Open 6 A.M. to 8 P.M., Sunday through
Thursday; 6 A.M. to 10 P.M., Friday and
Saturday.

Usery Mountain Recreation Area
(480) 984-0032
Entry fee.
Call for camping fees. Open 6 A.M. to 8 P.M.,
Sunday through Thursday; 6 A.M. to 10 P.M.,
Friday and Saturday.

Arizona State Parks
www.pr.state.az.us/parklist.html
Arizona State Parks Department,
(602) 542-4174.

Lost Dutchman State Park
(480) 982-4485
Entry fee.
Camping. Visitor center.

Superstition Wilderness
www.fs.fed.us/r3/tonto/recreation/wilderness/
supersti/super.htm
Tonto National Forest, Supervisor's Office,
2324 East McDowell Road, Phoenix, AZ;
(602) 225-5200; TTY, (602) 225-5395.

Mesa Ranger District
(480) 610-3300
Daily use fee at Peralta and First Water
trailheads. Call for information on recreation,
regulations, fees.

Tucson Backyard Hikes

**Sabino Canyon, Bear Canyon,
and Mount Lemmon**
www.fs.fed.us/r3/coronado/scrd/
Coronado National Forest, Supervisor's Office,
300 West Congress Street, Tucson, AZ;
(520) 670-4552.

Santa Catalina Ranger District
(520) 749-8700 — (also TDD)
Call for directions, regulations, fees, parking
pass for most recreation facilities on Mount
Lemmon and for Sabino Canyon parking lot.

Saguaro National Park
www.nps.gov/sagu/

Tucson Mountain Unit (Saguaro West)
(520) 733-5158
No entry fee. No camping.

Rincon Mountain District (Saguaro East)
(520) 733-5153 — also TDD
Entrance fee.
Backcountry camping all year with no-fee permit. Bring water.

Starr Pass Trail
www.co.pima.az.us/pksrec/home2/home2.html
Pima County Natural Resources, Parks and Recreation Department, 5955 Camino de la Tierra, Tucson, AZ 85741; (520) 740-2690.
Note: Phone number may change in 2002.

Arizona State Parks
Catalina State Park
(520) 628-5798
Entry fee.
Camping fee. Equestrian center, visitor center.

Prescott Backyard Hikes

Thumb Butte, Granite Mountain Wilderness, Spruce Mountain, and West Spruce Mountain
www.fs.fed.us/r3/prescott/
Prescott National Forest, Supervisor's Office/Bradshaw Ranger District, 344 South Cortez Street, Prescott, AZ;
(928) 771-4700
(928) 771-4708 — TTY/TDD
Call for directions, regulations, fees. Parking fees at several day-use areas and trailheads, including Thumb Butte family area and trailhead.

Flagstaff & Sedona Backyard Hikes

San Francisco Peaks, Lockett Meadow, Inner Basin, Kachina Trail, and Mount Elden
www.fs.fed.us/r3/coconino/rec_volcanic.html
Coconino National Forest, Supervisor's Office, 2323 East Greenlaw Lane, Flagstaff, AZ;
(928) 527-3600.

Peaks Ranger District
(928) 526-0866
Call for information on recreation, directions, regulations, fees.

Oak Creek, Brins Mesa Trail, Long Canyon Trail, A.B. Young Trail, Bell Rock, and Marg's Draw Trail
www.fs.fed.us/r3/coconino/rec_redrock.html
Coconino National Forest.

Sedona Ranger District
(928) 282-4119
Call for directions, regulations, fees, Red Rock Pass for parking; Red Rock Pass Program information at www.redrockcountry.org/.
(See Chapter 7.)

Walnut Canyon National Monument
www.nps.gov/waca/
(928) 526-3367
Entry fee.

Observatory Mesa Trail
www.flagstaff.az.gov
Maps for Flagstaff Urban Trails System (FUTS) sold at Flagstaff Parks and Recreation, 211 West Aspen Avenue, Flagstaff, AZ; (928) 779-7690.

opposite page: A hundred yards below the maple and fir grove where it emerges as a spring, Horton Creek spills over a log at the Highline Trail crossing.
NICK BERENZENKO

Want to hear the bad news first? The days of the mountain man are over. We continue to seek out that one spot where no one else has stood before, but just around the next bend in the canyon we find a discarded pair of boots, a broken flashlight, and a ballooned-up baggie of rotten hotdogs. Somebody *has* been here already.

Too many backcountry users feel that nature is a sort of omnipotent garbage disposal. It is not. Gone are the days when you could pitch camp with little regard for the environment or those who followed in your footsteps.

Now for the good news.

Arizona's backcountry and wilderness still live, in spite of sprawl and carelessness, and their treasures — fresh air, bird song, solitude, wildlife, and natural magnificence — are readily accessible to us and our children. What better way to learn the value of the outdoors than to pack up the family for a day of fresh air and wild spaces.

We don't have to live in regret, mourning an untouched land, completely without civilization, that we never had a chance to see. Let's get out and enjoy the backcountry that's been preserved just a hop, skip, and a jump from our driveways. We can make our active, respectful appreciation part of the legacy for the generations to come.

Welcome to this small selection of Arizona trails. There are so many to choose from, but these will give you a sense of the many other easily reached outings out there for people of all ages.

Horton Creek Trail

Fall is feast season in the mountains — gardeners savor fresh-picked vegetables, and mule deer stuff themselves with acorns and berries. But fall also serves a visual feast. Inconspicuous trees suddenly decorate themselves in crimson or gold, and normally drab shrubbery turns cranberry red.

One route to rich fall color is popular Horton Creek Trail northeast of Payson in late October to early November. This 4-mile trek (one way) begins at the end of the creek, just a short distance below the foot of the Mogollon Rim at the point where Horton Creek empties into Tonto Creek.

The trail's first half-mile displays purplish sumac and other colorful leaves, but no water — rocks bury the creek here. Only after crossing a fenceline do you find the stream running, complete with darting trout and gurgling sounds. Trail and creek then parallel each other the rest of the way.

Walking this trail, tracing an old wagon road toward the base of the Rim, looks fairly easy. But the route is deceptive, gaining more than 1,000 feet without ever appearing to climb. Your mind doesn't notice any major slope, but your legs feel as though they're plodding through deep sand. Luckily, flashes of color along the trail distract you from gravity's inconveniences.

A Virginia creeper stitches scarlet spirals around a dead gray tree trunk. Overhead, thick grapevines drape golden leaves along Douglas fir branches. Even the lowly poison ivy entices with its ruby red leaves and stems.

above: The falls at Horton Spring gladden this hiker.
NICK BERENZENKO

But the most serious color begins about 2 miles up from the trailhead. Here stand the first good groves of maples, swaying like bright party streamers against the backdrop of a dark forest.

While maples are not physically imposing, their leaves contain a variety of pigments that can range from pale flamingo to intense rose. They reveal it in their own time, too. One tree in mid-October might flush entirely pink. Another might wait until early November, then light up like a 40-foot torch — green on the bottom, yellow in the middle, flame red on top.

Four miles from the trailhead, Horton Creek Trail meets the Highline Trail, a long-distance thoroughfare. Just beyond, a shady hollow holds the headwaters of Horton Creek.

Listen and you'll locate the source of all you've seen: Horton Spring. This little gem, tucked in the rocks 20 or 30 feet above the stream, splashes out from the base of the Mogollon Rim. — *Rick Heffernon*

- **How To Get There:** Horton Creek Trail can be reached entirely by pavement. Drive 17 miles east of Payson on State Route 260. Turn left just past Kohl's Ranch onto Forest Service Road 289. Go 1 mile, cross a small bridge over Tonto Creek, and find the Horton Creek Picnic Site immediately on your left. Park and walk back across the bridge into the Upper Tonto Creek Campground. The trail starts there, dropping down to Horton Creek in the first few yards.
- **Elevation:** 5,300 to 6,700 feet.
- **Mileage:** 8 miles round trip.
- **Seasons:** April to November.
- **Maps:** USGS Promontory Butte quadrangle; Tonto National Forest map.
- **Nearest Supply Point:** Payson.
- **Backcountry Information:** Because of a harmful protozoan (*Giardia*) often in the water, do not drink untreated water. This hike gets hot in warm weather, so take enough water along. Hikers should yield right of way to trail stock.

Sugarloaf Mountain/Chiricahua National Monument

The payoff — a jungle of rocks — seems almost too generous for so short a ramble to the summit of Sugarloaf Mountain. Just below me to the south thrust the fantastic formations — Totem Pole, Big Balanced Rock, Punch and Judy — of Chiricahua National Monument's Heart of Rocks. I can see the elongated scoop of the Turkey Creek Caldera, an extinct volcano that 25 million years ago belched hot gases and fiery ash that heaped to a depth of some 2,000 feet. Carved by eons of wind and water, this hardened ash now forms the balanced rocks, spires, and minarets I'm seeing.

To the north stands another impressive rockscape, Cochise Head, shaped like the face of a reclining man — domed forehead, square jaw, prominent nose, and a tall pine for an eyelash. I can see forever, east to the peaks and ridges of the Animas Mountains along the Continental Divide in New Mexico, and west, far across Arizona's Sulphur Springs Valley to the Dragoon Mountains and beyond.

Our adventures began in the visitor center's parking lot. Before we drove to the trailhead, a troop of about 20 coatimundis emerged from the forest to forage in the dry bed of Bonita Creek. Holding their long tails erect, the young coatis ignored us and searched for acorns, lizards, and insects among overturned rocks. But the adults, particularly two large males, hunted on the perimeters, careful to stay between us and their young.

The coatis absorbed our attention for a good half hour before we left for the trailhead. The trail, 1 mile long and 500 feet in elevation gain, let us hike at a leisurely pace. After a short distance, we came to a small tunnel carved by Civilian Conservation Corps workers back in the 1930s. Along the way, we found many places to stop and enjoy the scenery.

Manzanita, piñon pine, juniper, and various oaks — including the Toumey oak with its small leathery bluish-green leaves — embellished the slopes. Evergreen and

shrublike, the Toumey oak helps prevent hillside erosion and provides dense shelter for small mammals and birds.

At the summit, we saw the Sugarloaf fire-lookout cabin, also built by CCC workers more than 60 years ago. In summer, the fire lookout is occupied by a fire watcher who monitors lightning strikes in the Chiricahua Mountains. Remember, the cabin is someone's home, so knock if you want to visit. — *Tom Dollar*

above: Its mask giving away its identity as a relative of the raccoon, this coatimundi clambers down a rock face as it forages for food.
MARTY CORDANO

opposite page: Hefty rock spires stand like an attentive crowd below Sugarloaf Mountain's summit.
MARTY CORDANO

- **How To Get There:** Take Interstate 10 south from Tucson 120 miles, exit at Willcox, and drive 36 miles on State Route 186 to the monument. From the visitor center, take the Bonita Canyon Scenic Drive as it curves north to east to south. At the junction, take the right fork that turns sharply northwest and drive to the Sugarloaf trailhead. Park in the lot on the north side of the road.
- **Elevation:** 6,810 feet at the trailhead; 7,310 feet at the summit.
- **Mileage:** 2 miles round trip.
- **Seasons:** Year round, but allow for snow in winter and daily thunderstorms from July through September.
- **Maps:** USGS Cochise Head quadrangle.
- **Nearest Supply Point:** Willcox (no food services, gas stations, or lodging in the monument itself).
- **Backcountry Information:** Campsites are available (fee, no reservations) in the Bonita Canyon campground only; no backcountry camping elsewhere.

Woods Canyon Lake

"The chipmunks are so bold," exclaims amateur artist Rita Goldner. "One jumped into the easel's tray, grabbed a pencil, and ate it." At Woods Canyon Lake, the chipmunks grow plump as guinea pigs — though not normally on a diet of art supplies.

The 52-acre lake rests at 7,500 feet atop the Mogollon Rim's precipitous sandstone brow. A popular part of the Apache-Sitgreaves National Forests, it offers seven developed campgrounds, where desert-dwellers seek refuge from the summer heat.

But escaping the crowds is easy on the flat 5-mile trail around the lake, an ideal family hike. A few downed trees and the lack of trail signs offer the only obstacles. Getting lost is not a worry, though; the lake is always nearby, and the path hugs the shoreline most of the way.

Begin at the Spillway Campground on the lake's southeast edge and continue across the dam at the eastern end. For the first 3 miles, the trail meanders through open, sunlit stands of ponderosas, Gambel oaks, and aspens. Indian paintbrush blossoms glow fluorescent-orange and western dayflowers unfurl deep-blue crests into the breeze. The miles pass easily on this longest section of the hike, past grassy meadows that invite you to picnic.

Near the lake's upper end, beaver-gnawed tree stumps dot the shore. Frowsy kingfishers sit atop the bony arms of snags, surveying the water for unwary fish. Several times the trail leads into long, secluded coves. In these pockets, you may find yourself lazing for a while to watch a cloud drift overhead or a cut-leaf coneflower sway in the cool breeze.

As the path rounds the upper end of the lake, the forest changes dramatically from dry and open to a denser, wetter world of dark Douglas fir, limber pine, and white fir. Old-man's-beard lichen flows from every branch. The old-growth forest provides cooling shade, and a thick fur of green moss coats every rock and fallen log. Carpets of wild strawberries, Canada violets, and red skyrockets vie for attention.

A half mile from the Rocky Point Picnic Area, the path joins the Nature Trail, a 1-mile hike from the picnic area, to a limestone sinkhole, and back. The lake hike ends at the Rocky Point parking lot. Shuttle back to the Spillway parking lot or hike a last half mile to close the loop. — *Scott Parrish*

■ **How To Get There:** From Payson, drive east on State Route 260 for 32 miles and turn left onto Forest Service Road 300. Drive 3.5 miles and turn right onto FR 105. Drive .75 mile to the Spillway Campground parking lot. For a shuttle hike, continue driving 1 mile northwest, past Aspen Campground and the general store, to the Rocky Point Picnic Area parking lot.

above: Regularly stocked with rainbow trout and encircled by a picturesque hiking trail, 52-acre Woods Canyon Lake provides a popular high-country destination.
NICK BEREZENKO
opposite page: Mist rises above the lake at dawn.
NICK BEREZENKO

- **Elevation:** 7,500 feet.
- **Mileage:** Flat 5-mile loop.
- **Seasons:** April through October.
- **Maps:** USGS Woods Canyon quadrangle; Apache-Sitgreaves National Forests map.
- **Nearest Supply Points:** Payson, Heber, Overgaard.
- **Backcountry Information:** Guided nature walks begin at 10 A.M. each Saturday, Memorial Day through Labor Day. Lake water is undrinkable. Carry plenty of water.

Kinder Crossing

More than 100 years have passed since R.C. Kinder's sheep waded East Clear Creek at his namesake crossing below Blue Ridge Reservoir in the heart of Mogollon Rim country. Now, the lug-soled boots of hikers and fishermen track Kinder Crossing Trail 19, a one-way hike of .75 mile or 1.5 miles, depending on your preference.

East Clear Creek slips between terraced limestone cliffs. Thickets of willow and alder frame somnolent pools, and an occasional trout surfaces to inhale its insect lunch. An easy access into the 600-foot-deep chasm along Kinder Crossing Trail appears at the end of Forest Service Road 95T and heads northeast down an easy slope conveniently stacked with steps of pitted limestone and gnarled roots. Steller's jays flash blue among the trees, and hawks pirouette overhead. After about 200 yards, the stream comes into view to the right. The track descends gently over bony limestone rubble and through a shaded saddle where footprints of deer, elk, and humans mingle.

After the saddle, instead of the route shown on the USGS map, the trail drops off steeply to the right. Long, angled slabs of sandstone give purchase for hiking boots on a series of tightly wound, well-engineered switchbacks.

Near the end of the .75-mile trip, roughly 100 feet separates the trail and stream. A large, dark pool broods below a ledge overgrown with pines, firs, and oaks. Outcrops of layered sandstone peek from the grassy slope. Underfoot a hematite-encrusted section of sandstone leaves the impression you're walking on a pavement of iron.

The trail reaches the stream at an elevated bench covered by mighty ponderosa pines. The path continues downstream to the confluence of Yaeger Canyon and crosses at the head of a long, shallow pool formed by a large sandstone abutment that juts into the stream. Relentless water and persistent time have eaten through the rock, creating an algae-covered spillway into the next large pool. Crayfish tank up the slick ramp, struggling to reach the top and mostly sliding back down. Most day hikers stop for lunch and a swim here and then head back out the way they came.

But adventurous types continue along the trail and cross the canyon — if they're armed with good route-finding skills and the appropriate topo maps. From the pool on, no cairns or blazes mark the way. This trail section heads downstream for another .75 mile over gravel bars dotted with willows, alders, and wildflowers. Beavers inhabit some of the long pools. Then the trail turns east up a long, sloping ridge to connect with FR 137. — *Scott Parrish*

above: Ponderosa pine-covered hillsides and narrow canyons greet the adventurous hiker who makes the trek to Kinder Crossing on East Clear Creek. NICK BEREZENKO

- **How To Get There:** From Payson, drive 50 miles north on State Route 87 to the Blue Ridge Ranger Station. Just past the ranger station, take the first right onto Forest Service Road 95 and drive 4.1 miles to FR 95T, turn left and follow the road for .6 of a mile to the Kinder Crossing Trail 19 sign at a fork in the road. Four-wheel-drive vehicles can continue for another .1 of a mile to the right to the actual trailhead.
- **Elevation:** 6,460 to 7,000 feet.
- **Mileage:** .75 mile or 1.5 miles, one way.
- **Seasons:** May to October.
- **Maps:** USGS Blue Ridge Reservoir quadrangle; Forest Service map for Coconino National Forest.
- **Nearest Supply Point:** Payson.
- **Backcountry Information:** To do the second half of the hike along the unmarked portion of the trail, check current trail conditions and carry the USGS Blue Ridge Reservoir topo map.

Bill Williams Mountain

For all practical purposes, you can drive to the top of 9,256-foot-high Bill Williams Mountain on a narrow, twisting road which corkscrews up the southern flank to the lookout and radio towers crowded onto its small, forested summit. However, the hiking trail leading to the summit gives you a fine taste of what it was like when mountain man Bill Williams trapped the area in the mid-1800s. Appropriately called the Bill Williams Trail, it's an excellent day hike from spring through fall.

You can reach the trailhead by driving west from downtown Williams on Bill Williams Avenue about 1 mile; turn left and go along the frontage road to the turnoff to the ranger station. Follow the signs to the trailhead. It's a stout, 2,000-foot climb in 3 miles up the north side of Bill Williams Mountain. The well-marked trail parallels the upper fork of West Cataract Creek through the aspens and Douglas fir to a fine lunch spot just before you reach the summit road. Always check with the Williams/Forest Service Visitor Center about fire danger.

Buckskin Mountain State Park

In the low, hot desert along the Colorado River near Parker Dam, 11 miles north of the city of Parker on State Route 95, Buckskin Mountain State Park has three developed trails — Wedge Hill, Lightning Bolt, and Buckskin. They are about .5, 1, and 2.5 miles long, respectively. These trails ascend steep bluffs to the mesa top and overlooks of the river.

below: Water recreation on the Colorado River is a popular attraction at Buckskin Mountain State Park.
LES DAVID MANEVITZ
opposite page: Surviving remnants of an ancient volcanic cataclysm, the rock formations in Chiricahua National Monument's Heart of the Rocks surround Cochise Head (foreground).
LARRY ULRICH

Chiricahua National Monument

There is great year-round hiking on well-maintained trails and the visitor center can give directions to spectacular hikes lasting from a few hours to all day. Here are just a couple. Day use only.

Echo Canyon Trail — The Echo Canyon Trail wanders down through an Alice-in-Wonderland labyrinth of hoodoos, balanced rocks, and narrow passages. In this maze, pinnacles and spires stand like chessmen, sculpted out of volcanic rock layers formed by an eruption millions of years ago. The trail starts at the Echo Canyon parking area. A nice loop trip of 3.5 miles takes you down Echo Canyon Trail and returns by Hailstone Trail through Rhyolite Canyon. However you climb out of the canyon, it's steep and can be hot in summer.

Heart of Rocks Trail — Some of the most distinctive rock formations and inspiring views in Chiricahua National Monument are seen along Heart of Rocks Trail. Unlike many other trails that take you into canyons, the 7-mile-round-trip trail is carved into the top of a mesa. It starts at the Massai Point parking area. This is an exhilarating full-day hike. Bring plenty of water.

Hualapai Mountain Park

The Hualapai Mountains, south of Kingman, provide magnificent vistas of the surrounding basin-and-range landscape of northwestern Arizona. From the campground at about 7,000 feet, three relatively easy trails meander up Hualapai, Hayden, and Aspen peaks. A short trail climbs Hualapai Peak at 8,417 feet and a 2.7-mile trail reaches Hayden Peak. Built in 1981, the developed Hualapai Trail begins at 6,314 feet elevation and reaches 8,239 feet at Aspen Peak. From the top, one can see four states — Utah, Nevada, California, and of course, Arizona. Other trails are marked on the USGS Hualapai Peak and Dean Peak quadrangle maps.

From U.S. Route 93 on the east end of Kingman, take the Hualapai Mountain Road about 12 miles up Sawmill Canyon to Hualapai Mountain Park. Or take Exit 51 south off Interstate 40. Take Stockton Hill Road south until it becomes Hualapai Mountain Road. Go 14 miles to the park. Heavy winter snowfalls may require four-wheel drive or chains.

opposite page: Blue shadows finger the valley stretched below Hualapai Mountain Park and Getz Peak. DAVID H. SMITH

Lower Paria Canyon/Lees Ferry

If you're not inclined to trek through Paria Canyon, Lees Ferry is a great place to explore similar terrain for an hour or a full day. The towering Vermilion Cliffs dominate the scene.

A short hike along the Paria River passes the old cemetery and the remains of Lonely Dell, the farm established by John Doyle Lee when he founded the ferry across the Colorado River in 1871. The Church of Jesus Christ of Latter-day Saints (Mormons) used this route for its people to colonize Arizona from Utah. A 1-mile hike up the river from the boat ramp takes you along the old wagon road, past Lee's fort building and the wreck of a steamboat.

Lees Ferry is about 15 miles downriver from Glen Canyon Dam. From Bitter Springs on U.S. Route 89, go north 14 miles on U.S. 89A until you cross Navajo Bridge. Go about 300 yards, and the Lees Ferry turnoff is on your right.

Mount Baldy

At 11,590 feet in the White Mountains, Mount Baldy is one of the highest mountains in Arizona. The extinct volcano is sacred to White Mountain Apaches and figures in the lore of other tribes. A forest of Engelmann spruce, blue spruce, and Douglas fir harbors elk, beaver, golden-mantled ground squirrels, Audubon's warbler, gray jays, and red-breasted nuthatches.

From the trailhead off State Route 273, the trail meanders through alpine meadows and along the West Fork of the Little Colorado River. In about 7 miles, it climbs from 9,300 feet to near timberline at 11,200 feet. The last mile to the top of

above: The Vermilion Cliffs, near Lees Ferry, are northern Arizona's chameleons. Weather and time of day may shade them in bleached pinks and peaches, deep rusty reds, or — under a cloudy June sunset — rich lavenders and violets. GARY LADD
opposite page: In the Mount Baldy Wilderness, the West Fork Trail tantalizes with the triple treat of shady forests, grassy meadows, and the Little Colorado River. WILLARD CLAY

above: Near Mount Wrightson's summit, a hiker on the Crest Trail swings past ponderosa pine snags.
PETER NOEBELS

Mount Baldy is on the Fort Apache Indian Reservation. Hiking in this sacred area is forbidden.

Summer through fall is the best time to explore the Mount Baldy Wilderness. It is always cool. Thunderstorms develop quickly.

Take State Route 260 east of McNary to State 273, the Big Lake road. Drive south about 8 miles to the trailhead sign for the West Baldy Trail. This trailhead is about 1 mile north and east of the old one at Sheeps Crossing.

Mount Wrightson

At the head of Madera Canyon beginning the climb up Mount Wrightson, you already are in ponderosa pine forest at 5,500 feet elevation. You have a choice of the Old Baldy Trail or the newer Mount Wrightson Trail. Old Baldy is shorter, but steeper. You might want to try this combination: Start on the Mount Wrightson Trail, which leaves from the lower end of Roundup picnic area parking lot and follows a gorge 3.7 miles to Josephine Saddle. Old Baldy also crosses this saddle, and is a good way to travel the next 1.6 miles to Baldy Saddle. You pass dependable Sprung and Bellows springs along the way. The final mile to 94,53-foot Mount Wrightson is an exposed trail, providing awesome views of southern Arizona.

You can climb Wrightson year-round, but high mountains create their own weather. Bring more clothing and food than you might think you need.

To get there, take the Continental Exit from Interstate 19, about halfway between Tucson and Nogales. Follow the signs 13 miles to the head of Madera Canyon, where there are Coronado National Forest campgrounds and picnic sites.

Organ Pipe Cactus National Monument

Quitobaquito is a special place for both its natural history and for its place in human history. It is the most dependable source of water between Sonoyta, Sonora, and the Colorado River. It is a milepost on a route known as El Camino del Diablo, or Devil's Highway. The Camino was a southern trade route for Indians traveling from Arizona and Sonora to the Colorado River and southern California. Many sleeping circles, bedrock metates, and petroglyphs are found along this trail of the ancient people. In 1540, Melchior Diaz, one of Coronado's lieutenants, ventured across. Father Eusebio Francisco Kino followed the route in 1699, and eventually pioneers followed the Camino in wagons to bypass the absolutely dry, active sand desert to the south.

West of Quitobaquito, water, if there is any, is found in depressions in bedrock, called tinajas, which trap rainfall. The tinajas are scant and undependable water holes.

Several trails in the monument offer close looks at the beauty of the desert. From shortest to longest:

Quitobaquito Nature Trail — (.5-mile round-trip). One of the most fascinating, refreshing, and enjoyable short hikes you will take anywhere. Starting at Milepost 20 on Puerto Blanco Drive, this well-marked trail provides an excellent introduction to Organ Pipe's rich flora and fauna. Many different species of birds have been sighted at this oasis. Bring your binoculars.

Campground Perimeter Trail — (1-mile loop). This trail makes an ideal leisurely walk to start or end the day.

Desert View Nature Trail — (1.2-mile loop). Starting at the group campground parking lot, this circular route provides some delightful vistas of the monument and the Sonoyta Valley all the way into Mexico.

Victoria Mine Trail — (4.5-mile round-trip). Starting at the south end of the campground, this hike takes you over rolling desert terrain to the monument's richest and oldest gold and silver mine.

Alamo Canyon — If you want a longer hike, here's a good one. Immediately north of Alamo Wash Bridge, about 8 miles south of Why on State Route 85, is a 3-mile dirt road that takes you eastward to four primitive campsites at the mouth of

Alamo Canyon. Although there are no defined trails, this open desert country provides a great opportunity for cross-country treks; take the USGS Mount Ajo and Tillotson Peak quadrangles. A casual hike to explore magnificent Alamo Canyon can easily take all day. On the alluvial plain at the base of the Ajo Mountains, brittlebush and spring wildflowers put on a spectacular display in early March during wetter years. A permit is required from the visitor center for overnight stays.

Petrified Forest National Park and the Painted Desert

These expansive badlands let you enjoy cross-country hikes and shorter nature walks. Go in spring and fall, when it's not so hot. The best introductory hikes are within the park, shortest to longest:

Agate House Trail — (.5-mile round-trip). Discover the prehistoric Indian dwellings made of petrified wood.

opposite page: For centuries, the spring at Quitobaquito has quenched the thirst of desert tribes, wandering travelers, desert bighorn, and diverse species of birds, like these coots. JACK DYKINGA **below:** Lying like split logs for a giant's hearth, mineralized tree trunk fragments lie across Jasper Forest's plain in the Petrified Forest National Park. DAVID MUENCH

Crystal Forest Trail — (.5-mile loop). All sizes of petrified wood fragments, from chips to whole logs, cover the terrain.

Blue Mesa Trail — (.8-mile loop). Hike off the mesa into the blue, gray, and brown arroyos. You'll think you're on the moon. This is perhaps the park's most dramatic display of erosion.

Long Log Trail — (.8-mile loop). You can gawk at the petrified remains of a giant logjam without embarrassment — some logs are 170 feet long, and it's the world's largest concentration of petrified wood.

Painted Desert — These day hikes tend to be longer; if you go off trail, you'll need a permit (no fee). From the park's northwest section, a trail leads into the Painted Desert. Starting at Kachina Point, you can go north across Lithodendron Wash about 2 miles to the Black Forest or 6 miles to Chinde Mesa.

There is no drinking water, so take plenty. It's easy to get lost, so take a compass and maps; the USGS Pilot Rock, Chinde Mesa, North Mill Well, Little Lithodendron Tank, Kachina Point, Pinta Point, Carrizo Butte, Adamana, Padilla Tank, and Agate House quadrangles cover the entire park (they don't note the Painted Desert, but refer to the Petrified Forest National Wilderness).

Enter at the park's north entrance on Interstate 40, 25 miles northeast of Holbrook, or at its south entrance southeast of Holbrook on U.S. Route 180. The three visitor centers stay open all year: Painted Desert Visitor Center, at Interstate 40, 8 A.M. to 5 P.M.; Painted Desert Inn Visitors Center, 2 miles from the north entrance, 8 A.M. to 4 P.M.; and Rainbow Forest Museum, at the south entrance, 8 A.M. to 5 P.M.

Sycamore Canyon/Nogales

There are several Sycamore Canyons in Arizona. Not to be confused with a better-known Sycamore, which empties into the Verde Valley, the southern Sycamore Canyon is west of Nogales. Running generally north to south, the canyon extends 5 miles to the Mexican border. As you walk through shallow pools, the intermittent stream meanders past pinnacles and cliffs of volcanic rock rising above a lush canyon bottom. With care, and a little luck, you might see a rare coppery-tailed trogon.

Take Interstate 19 about 6 or 7 miles north of Nogales, turn west on State Route 289 for 10 miles to Pena Blanca Lake, then continue another 10 miles on a narrow, graded gravel road to Sycamore Canyon. Check out the Coronado National Forest map or the USGS Kino Springs, Cumero Canyon, and Harshaw quadrangles.

above: Canyon de Chelly is home to Navajo families who herd their sheep and harvest their gardens and peach orchards.
DAVID MUENCH

White House Ruin Trail/
Canyon de Chelly National Monument

The streaks of blue-black varnish across the massive sandstone cliffs of Canyon de Chelly draw your attention to the pueblo ruin (not to be confused with the White House ruin at the head of Paria Canyon). If you are at the White House overlook on the canyon's opposite rim (reached by road from Chinle), the view of White House beckons you closer. A trail leads 500 feet down into the canyon and across the streambed to the base of the cliff dwelling ruins. It is an enjoyable hike and the only part of Canyon de Chelly accessible without an authorized Navajo guide. In the fall, cottonwoods along the canyon bottom blaze with color.

You don't need to buy a permit or pay a fee to hike the White House Ruin Trail, but you will if you want to hike or drive any other route into this national monument on the Navajo Nation.

When You Go

**Horton Creek Trail and
the Mogollon Rim**
www.fs.fed.us/r3/tonto/
Tonto National Forest, Supervisor's Office,
2324 East McDowell Road, Phoenix, AZ;
(602) 225-5395
(602) 225-5200 — TTY

> Payson Ranger District
> (928) 474-7900
> Call for recreation information, directions,
> regulations, fees.

**Woods Canyon Lake
and Mount Baldy Wilderness**
www.fs.fed.us/r3/asnf/
Apache-Sitgreaves National Forests, Supervisor's
Office, P.O. Box 640, Springerville, AZ;
(928) 333-4301
(928) 333-6292 — TTY

> Black Mesa Ranger District
> (Woods Canyon Lake)
> (928) 535-4481
> (928) 535-3213 — TTY
> Call for information on recreation, directions,
> regulations, fees.

> Springerville Ranger District (Mount Baldy)
> (928) 333-4372
> (928) 333-6618 — TTY
> Call for recreation information, directions,
> regulations, fees. No bikes in the wilderness.

Kinder Crossing Trail
www.fs.fed.us/r3/coconino/rec_mogollon.html
Coconino National Forest, Supervisor's Office,
2323 East Greenlaw Lane, Flagstaff, AZ;
(928) 527-3600.

> Happy Jack Information Center at Clint's Well
> Milepost 290, State Route 87
> (928) 477-2172
> Open daily with maps, brochures, regulation
> information.

Bill Williams Mountain
www.fs.fed.us/r3/kai/recreation/trwc.html
Kaibab National Forest, Supervisor's Office,
800 South 6th Street, Williams, AZ;
(928) 635-8200.

> Williams/Forest Service Visitor Center
> 200 West Railroad Avenue
> Williams, AZ
> (800) 863-0546 (also TTY)
> (928) 635-4707 or 4061 (also TTY)
> Cooperative visitor center; 8 A.M. to 5 P.M.
> daily, weekends. Maps, information, exhibits.

> Williams Ranger District
> (928) 635-5600
> Call for information on recreation,
> directions, regulations, fees.

Arizona State Parks
www.pr.state.az.us/parkhtml/buckskin.html
Arizona State Parks Department,
(602) 542-4174.

> Buckskin Mountain State Park
> (928) 667-3231
> Entry fee. Camping, boating, fishing.
> Accessible rest rooms. Marina store.

Canyon de Chelly
www.nps.gov/cach/
Chinle, AZ 86503
(928) 674-5500
White House Trail is the only one you can hike
without a guide, permit, or fee.

Hualapai Mountain Park
www.hualapaimountainpark.com/
Mohave County Parks Department
(928) 754-7204

> Hualapai Mountain Park
> (928) 757-0915
> Camping. No reservations.

Lees Ferry and Lower Paria Canyon
www.nps.gov/glca/lferry.htm

Glen Canyon Recreation Area, Headquarters
(928) 608-6200

Carl Hayden Visitor Center, U.S. 89, Page, AZ
(928) 608-6404

24-Hour Emergency
(800) 582-4351

Lees Ferry Ranger Station
(928) 355-2234

Navajo Bridge Interpretive Center,
U.S. 89A near Lees Ferry
Daily, mid-April to October, 9 A.M. to 5 P.M.;
weekends only, early April and November,
10 A.M. to 4 P.M.

Mount Wrightson and Sycamore Canyon
www.fs.fed.us/r3/coronado/nrd/nogo.htm
Coronado National Forest, Supervisor's Office,
300 West Congress Street, Tucson, AZ;
(520) 670-4552.

Nogales Ranger District
(520) 281-2296
Call for seasonal restrictions, use fees.
No bikes in the wilderness.

Petrified Forest National Park
www.nps.gov/pefo/
(928) 524-6228
Entry fee, overnight backpacking permit (no
fee). Nearby communities offer all services.

Organ Pipe Cactus National Monument
www.nps.gov/orpi/
(520) 387-6849
Entry fee. Camping fee. Backcountry camping
with permit. Food, services, lodging in Ajo.

Sugarloaf Mountain
www.nps.gov/chir
Chiricahua National Monument
(520) 824-3560
Entry fee. Camping fees. No backcountry
camping. Supplies, services, lodging in Willcox.
Visitor center, campground fully accessible.

opposite page:
Turning aspens bugle winter's advance from the western slopes of the San Francisco Peaks outside of Flagstaff. Distant haze blurs the edges of Kendrick Peak beyond. TOM DANIELSEN

I first saw the San Francisco Peaks from a high school bus. We'd driven north that January day to ski Arizona's highest mountains. Getting out, I looked up and saw what I assumed was the tip of Humphreys Peak.

I broke trail, and my ski date, Ricarda, trudged behind, thinking I knew a quicker way up than using the chairlift like our classmates. In just a half-hour, though, dots spun before my eyes. Struggling to catch my breath in the thin air, I saw another ridge behind the "summit" — and another beyond that.

"Ricarda," I panted, "this is high enough for your first time out." She laughed, unaffected by the elevation, and said, "Let's ski."

I told her to do exactly as I did, even though the only time I'd ever skied was on snow from a giant ice machine in Phoenix.

"Watch," I said. I tucked into an FBI crouch, planted my poles into the icy crust, and pushed off . . . 10 feet down, my skis shot out from under me, and I exploded into the air like a rag doll. When I screeched to a halt, my poles hung in the trees and my skis had rocketed downslope alone.

I vowed never to *ski* down a mountain again. What I relished was the hike up the daunting slope, but Phoenix, about 1,100 feet above sea level, was no preparation for a 12,000-foot peak. Rather than suffering hypoxia and altitude sickness again, I decided to train gradually on lesser mountains until I could one day scale Humphreys.

This chapter's hikes aren't all alpine treks, but each is more challenging than the average family hike. Like me on my high school outing, you may find that you have a conditioning or learning curve on some trails and that others are a little remote for spending all day with younger children. — *John Annerino*

West Fork of Oak Creek

The West Fork of Oak Creek offers several hike options: a few hours or a full day from its lower end, or an arduous overnight bushwhack beginning on the plateau above, and ending where West Fork joins the main Oak Creek Canyon. The last option forces even experienced hikers to commit to a point-of-no-return situation, so we'll take the lower end, which is spectacle enough.

Much that is sought after on an Arizona jaunt comes together along the Mogollon Rim, a transition zone between the basin-and-range region to the south and the Colorado Plateau to the north.

In these canyons, plants of the lower zone — prickly pear cactus, agave, piñon pine, and juniper — meet ponderosa pine and Douglas fir. Where they converge with the rich streambed vegetation, the mixture is luxuriant.

Faulting allowed the canyons to break through the plateau's resistant cap of lava. Once through that cap, water carved the spectacular canyons through the softer, red layers of sedimentary rock below. Faulting and fracturing also made it possible for springs to feed the canyon streams today.

Where West Fork joins Oak Creek, the trail begins in an apple orchard near the old burned-out ruins of Mayhew Lodge. Towering sandstone cliffs form a cathedral-like entrance as you pass into what seems like another world.

A well-traveled path crisscrosses the creek. Just beyond this meadow, a long, shallow pool extends upstream from the first crossing. Water seeping from the sandstone overhang splashes into the pool. A larger splash might be a water ouzel, a gray bird like a large wren that dips underwater to run along the bottom to catch food. Listen for the canyon wren's distinctively clear whistle; watch for the bridled titmouse, yellow warbler, and Bullock's oriole.

Although the canyon of the West Fork twists and turns, essentially it runs east and west, dropping from the high country west of Oak Creek. Generally cool and damp, it shelters abundant fern and moss gardens. Tight clumps of horsetails, looking like green soda straws capped with crowns, grow on the muddy banks. One of the earliest land plants, horsetails grew in the ancient forests and swamps when these red rocks were first being formed. Dense stands of dogwood and boxwood edge the banks, adorned occasionally by yellow monkey flower. In the fall, the fire-red-to-brilliant-yellow of the turning big-tooth maples spark the canyon and its shadowy glens. Pines mix with deciduous trees over a forest floor of ferns and white violets.

Half-mile posts flank the trail for the first several miles. Just beyond the 2-mile mark, watch for a bare rock platform undercut by the stream. This is a great place for a snack or a snooze. Across the creek, somewhat hidden by the dense streamside vegetation, is a "wave cave," another overhang with a striking resemblance to a huge ocean wave. Water sculpted this, like many other alcoves and overhangs, when the stream was higher.

Not far beyond, the path becomes less defined. Zealous explorers can continue, but the route gets tangled in trees and brush. In some places you can wade in the creek to avoid the dense, tangled growth. Occasionally, the canyon is blocked by

opposite page:
Skirting a sharply vertical cliff in Oak Creek Canyon, a hiker balances with the help of his walking stick. Local custom suggests that returning hikers obligingly leave their sticks at the trailhead for the next visitors.
TOM BEAN

boulders, logjams, and deep, wall-to-wall pools. You have to climb or swim to get past these.

West Fork is a great day hike all year. Weekdays are less crowded than weekends. Camping and campfires are forbidden in the first 6 miles above the confluence with Oak Creek.

Because wading is unavoidable, it is most comfortable from late spring through the fall. Heavy wool socks help keep feet warmer during colder weather, even when wet. Rocks in the creek are usually slippery, especially when covered with slimy algae.

Flash flooding is the main danger. Canyon streams swell quickly when it storms. In the lower ends of the deep canyons, hikers may miss noticing localized summer thunderstorms a few miles up the drainage. It is important to check local weather forecasts before starting out. Take extra food and clothing in case you must wait out a storm and its flood waters, which usually pass in a few hours. We tend to underestimate the power of rushing water. Water knee-deep and flowing only a few miles per hour still can sweep a person away. — *Peter Kresan*

below: Sloshing through the West Fork of Oak Creek is a given on this refreshing route, so choose a season when you won't get chilled. TOM BEAN

above: Some of Oak Creek's curvaceously cut overhangs reflect perfectly in a mirrored pool's depths.
ROBERT G. McDONALD

■ **How To Get There:** The West Fork trailhead is 10.75 miles north of the Sedona junction of U.S. Route 89A and State Route 179. Take 89A through Oak Creek Canyon. Parking space is limited along 89A at the trailhead, but .2 of a mile farther up the canyon, a large parking lot is located off the west side of the road.

A paved path leads past a private home and down to the crossing of Oak Creek. Wade across the stream near the old stone buttresses which mark the site of a washed-out foot bridge. Then follow the path past the ruins of Mayhew Lodge and through the orchard to the mouth of West Fork.

■ **Primary Access:** U.S. Route 89A.

■ **Elevation:** 5,200 feet at the mouth of West Fork; 6,500 feet on the plateau above.

■ **Mileage:** Approximately 3 miles one way.

■ **Water:** More than enough, but purify.

■ **Seasons:** Late spring through early fall for the upper end.

■ **Maps:** USGS Dutton Hill, Wilson Mountain, Munds Park quadrangles; Coconino National Forest map.

■ **Nearest Supply Points:** Flagstaff and Sedona.

■ **Backcountry Information:** Day-use area parking lot charges a daily fee. Overnight backpacking or camping requires permits. No campfires allowed.

Bull Pasture/Organ Pipe Cactus National Monument

If you live in the Mexican state of Sonora, just a few miles south, Organ Pipe Cactus National Monument looks like your own backyard. But for the rest of us, it spreads a unique blanket of plants, strangely lush in the midst of a desert. Here it's virtually frost-free and gets enough summer rains for tropical plants to reach their northern limits. To the west, the land is too dry; to the east, too cold. So here grow smoke tree, senita cactus, limberbush, and the best population of organ pipe cactus in the United States.

After a wet winter, the bloom of brittlebush and annual wildflowers in February and March can set the scene aglow with color. Late summer thunderstorms bring more moisture, and the freshly green plants stand out against the stark volcanic cliffs of the Ajo Mountains.

Rising to 4,808 feet at Mount Ajo, the Ajos are the highest, most massive range in southwestern Arizona. They effectively deflect the warm, moist air from the Sea of Cortés high enough to cool and condense into rain.

Ajo Mountain Drive, a 21-mile loop road, provides access to viewpoints, trails, and cross-country hiking with spectacular views. As the loop road begins to parallel

above: Pampered by unexpectedly tropical temperatures in winter and drenching rains in summer, Organ Pipe Cactus National Monument looks like a wildly formidable garden. Brittlebush and ocotillo intersperse abundant organ pipe, saguaro, and jumping cholla cactus. GEORGE H.H. HUEY
opposite page: Hiking the Bull Pasture Trail is very dry recreation, even when the sunlit plants are verdant reminders of recent rain. TOM BEAN

the imposing front of the Ajos, look for a prominent cliff with a "window" framing the azure sky.

There is no finer display of organ pipe cactus in the monument than on the southwestern flank of the Ajo Mountains, along the trail to Bull Pasture. The trail is a 4-mile loop switchbacking up to Bull Pasture and back through Estes Canyon. Bull Pasture is at the end of a short but steep side trail. Each step opens up magnificent vistas of the basins and ranges in southwestern Arizona and New Mexico. Like layered shingles, the mountain ranges stack westward, one after another. Between them lie wide, somewhat desolate valleys or basins.

Like most ranges and basins in southern Arizona, the elevation differences of about 3,100 feet between Mount Ajo and the valley floor grew mostly from when these large crustal blocks shifted vertically during ancient earthquakes. Layers of brown lava and alternating tan and yellow volcanic tuffs tell yet another geologic story — of cataclysmic volcanic eruptions about 25 million years ago.

For spectacular views, there is nothing like being at the top above Bull Pasture. Mount Ajo's summit beckons anyone willing to hike cross-country. It's a very strenuous trek with some traverses along ridge crests. Constantly remind yourself not to climb up anything you couldn't safely get down. The topographical map for the park shows a spring just above Bull Pasture, but don't count on water. Except for Dripping Springs in the Puerto Blanco Mountains and Quitobaquito, local oases can't be counted on.

From your perch at the edge of Bull Pasture, the great expanse of stark mountains and desert valleys lies parched before you. Yet, surviving out there are bighorn sheep and pronghorn antelope. If you walk quietly, maybe you'll glimpse one. — *Peter Kresan*

opposite page:
The Ajo Mountains loom beyond blooming brittlebush, organ pipe and cholla cactus, and leafing ocotillo. Ocotillo looks like a cluster of twisted, bare sticks stuck in the ground, except when there's been rain — prompting tiny green leaves to sprout along each trunk's entire length — or when it's in bloom — and plume-like clusters of flowers tip each branch. WILLARD CLAY

- **How To Get There:** From Phoenix, drive south on U.S. Route 80 and State Route 85 140 miles; from Tucson, take State 86 and State 85 142 miles.
- **Primary Access:** Estes Canyon picnic area on Ajo Mountain Drive, via Bull Pasture.
- **Elevation:** 2,400 feet at Estes Canyon picnic area to 4,808 feet atop Mount Ajo.
- **Mileage:** Estes Canyon to Bull Pasture, 4.1 miles round trip. Approximately 4 miles one way to Mount Ajo.
- **Water:** Rangers recommend that hikers not use seasonal water anywhere in Organ Pipe unless it's an emergency because animals rely on it.
- **Escape Route:** Via Bull Pasture to Estes Canyon.
- **Seasons:** Late fall through early spring. Summer can be deadly.
- **Maps:** USGS Mount Ajo, Diaz Peak, Kino Peak, and Lukeville quadrangles or topographical map sold at visitor center.
- **Nearest Supply Points:** Gila Bend, Ajo, Lukeville, and Sells.
- **Backcountry Information:** No campfires. Overnight hiking by permit only. Bikes on scenic loop roads only. The trek up to Mount Ajo is an excellent day hike or overnighter, but make sure you can observe the route to the summit crest before leaving Bull Pasture. The route alongside the conical turrets, though longer, is probably safer. To spend the night on this incredible perch, there are several ledges suitable for two on the east-southeast side of the peak. Remember, it's farther from the Bull Pasture hiker register than it looks.

Cathedral Wash

The hikers stepped carefully along a ledge skirting an imposing outcropping. A few loose rocks ricocheted against the walls of the narrow wash before hitting bottom, a reminder that a misstep might land them 50 feet below. Following cairns along the route they must take to safely sidestep another pour-off in the wash, the hikers reached a wider, more comfortable spot on the ledge. From there, they hopped down a series of smaller ledges leading back into the wash's bottom.

Neither hair-raising nor a cakewalk, the 1.25-mile route down Cathedral Wash to the Colorado River near Lees Ferry makes a fun change of pace from a designated trail. Most of the routes in the Glen Canyon National Recreation Area, where the hike begins, require good route-finding skills, strenuous climbing, or dangerous trekking over slick-rock. Cathedral Wash, however, offers a challenge considered moderate enough for most people to enjoy.

Generally sharp and raspy, the Kaibab limestone walls at the route's beginning stand smooth and well-worn by flooding that has created a series of chutelike pour-offs. Staff at the Carl Hayden Visitor Center at Glen Canyon Dam warn hikers to stay away from the wash when there's any hint of rain. This is a hike for a sunny day; preferably in the dry, milder months of spring and fall.

A metal sign near the first pour-off designates the boundary of Grand Canyon National Park and informs hikers that permits are required for overnight use. From there, the walls grow as the route eventually drops a total of 200 feet. Arches appear, one near a set of utility wires strung across the rim of the canyon and one near the river. Strangely sculpted rocks peer into the canyon from its lip.

Hikers will continue to climb up and down ledges, ducking under low-hanging alcoves, and plodding across the sandy wash floor for about 1 mile — until they hear the roar of Cathedral Rapids at the Colorado River.

In spots near the Colorado, weaker Toroweap sandstone walls have caved in under the force of the river's erosion, creating an obstacle course of boulders for hikers to wind through.

The 45-degree water of the Colorado River makes a welcome destination on a hot day, and Paria Beach is a great place to relax with a riverside picnic lunch. — *Christine Maxa*

below: The Colorado River's nippy waters can soothe weary feet at the end of a warm day's hike.
DAVID H. SMITH
opposite page: Cathedral Canyon begins as a sandy wash at the foot of the Vermilion Cliffs.
DAVID H. SMITH

■ **How To Get There:** Cathedral Wash is west of Page and approximately 285 miles north of Phoenix, or about 140 miles north of Flagstaff. From Flagstaff, take U.S. Route 89 north toward Page until you reach the junction at Bitter Springs. There, take U.S. 89A to Lees Ferry Road, then drive 1 mile to the second turnout at Cathedral Rock. Walk just north of the turnout to Cathedral Wash, and head east (right) into the canyon to the Colorado River.

■ **Mileage:** 2.5 miles round trip.

■ **Seasons:** Spring and fall months, on dry, sunny days.

■ **Maps:** Topographical maps sold at Navajo Bridge visitor center.

■ **Nearest Supply Points:** Marble Canyon-Vermilion Cliffs community (limited) and Page, Arizona; Kanab, Utah.

■ **Backcountry Information:** Permits required for overnight use. Because of flash flood danger, do not hike at this wash (or any other) if rain threatens. Wear a hat and sunscreen. Hikers should be in good physical health since this is a remote location. Anyone with vertigo should not attempt the route.

above: Water has worked its will on Cathedral Canyon's undulating walls.
DAVID H. SMITH

Palm Canyon Trail

This kind of desert is not for everyone. In fact, the Kofa Wildlife Refuge, more than any other area of Arizona, may be closest to the image of a desert that someone coming from Ohio or Connecticut might have in mind.

Aside from the well-trod Palm Canyon Trail, there are no developed trails in this 663,700-acre refuge — just faint game trails and traces of Indian trade routes.

William Keiser described prospecting in the local mountain range in the 1890s: "An old Indian trail went over the mountain and going up the trail he [Charlie Eichelberger] discovered a small cave, and overhanging rock where the evidence showed that the Indians cooked there. . . . Where the smoke covered the wall he noticed some bright yellow spots — gold . . ."

Charlie and his grubstaking partner sold the find in 1897 for $250,000. It became the King of Arizona Mine. The initials KOFA stenciled on the crates of mine supplies replaced the former scatalogical name for the mountain range that once appeared on maps.

The rust-colored volcanic rocks, which stack up to form the Kofa Mountains, might remind one of a gigantic layer cake without icing. They rise dramatically from a broad valley, called La Posa Plain. The desert floor slopes gently to the abrupt mountain front and appears paved with a mosaic surface of interlocked pebbles and cobbles. This so-called desert pavement is formed as wind blows the fine dust away, leaving those fragments too big to be moved by the wind. These in turn protect the ground from further wind erosion. Some of the cobbles in the pavement are such a shiny blue-black that you might think the desert is littered with meteorites. But the shiny "desert varnish," formed by the precipitation of iron and manganese oxides, coats only the top sides of the pebbles.

Winter and spring are my favorite times to explore the Kofas. March can be windy, but the dust kicked up into the atmosphere creates spectacular sunsets. There are no dependable water holes, so bring plenty of water.

The Kofa Mountains contain the most extensive natural groves of *Washingtonia* palm trees in Arizona. These palms are in Palm Canyon and such adjacent canyons as Fishtail, Four Palms, and Old Palm. The sheer orange cliffs of Palm Canyon provide a dramatic setting for the grove. Cross-country hikes in these adjacent canyons might reward you with a glimpse of a desert bighorn sheep. One of my best sightings of a bighorn was one spring day in Fishtail Canyon. We decided to trek along the mountain front to the south in search of more palms. It was relatively easy going across the open desert, skirting the rugged mountain face. Beavertail prickly pear cactus were blooming, and occasionally a hummingbird would dive bomb my red day pack, perhaps thinking it was a huge ocotillo bloom.

Instead of entering Fishtail, as we had planned, we decided to quietly climb, unnoticed, the nose of a ridge at the entrance. It worked. From the ridge crest we spotted a beautiful ram with massive curled horns wandering along the canyon bottom. It was some time before he caught our scent and disappeared up the boulder-choked canyon.

Studies have shown that desert bighorns can go three to five days without water. Then they find moisture in tinajas, bedrock tanks that erosion has carved in the bottoms of the steep upper canyons. If you do discover tinajas, it is best not to disturb the bighorns' water supply, unless your need for water is dire. Desert bighorns usually travel in family groups, so if you spot one, look for others.

We got into Fishtail Canyon and worked our way through the dense brush lining the channel of the wash. It was like walking in a tunnel. Vines engulfed some of the larger palm trees, creating a promenade which contrasted sharply with the much browner desert just 100 feet away. At dusk, the hoot of a screech owl and the howl of coyotes out on the plain reminded us of other timorous inhabitants of the desert. — *Peter Kresan*

opposite page: As fantastically toothed as a goblin's grin, the Kofa Mountains jut from a desert floor littered with darkly varnished rocks and sparked with the surprise of brittlebush flowers. DAVID MUENCH

- **How To Get There:** Take U.S. Route 95 approximately 63 miles north of Yuma. Watch for the Palm Canyon sign indicating a junction with a dirt road. Turn left (east) on the Palm Canyon Road and go approximately 7.5 miles to the mouth of Palm Canyon. An easy to moderate hike for the first .5 mile, this is the most popular hike in the Kofas because it's the only place where Arizona's native palm trees grow in the natural habitat.
- **Primary Access:** Palm Canyon Road approximately 7.5 miles.
- **Elevation:** 2,200 feet at Palm Canyon parking lot.
- **Mileage:** Approximately .5 mile into Palm Canyon. Cross-country hiking mileage is at your discretion.
- **Seasons:** Late fall through early spring (wildflower season). Summer can be deadly.
- **Maps:** USGS Livingston Hills quadrangle. U.S. Fish and Wildlife map available in leaflet boxes at most entrances.
- **Nearest Supply Points:** Quartzsite and Yuma.
- **Backcountry Information:** No permit required. Fires allowed, but wood is scarce. Bikes on designated roads only. You may find tinajas (natural tanks) full after a rain. However, these are key water resources for the desert bighorn and should be used only in dire emergencies.

Temporal Gulch Trail

In the riparian, or streamside, area of southern Arizona's Temporal Gulch, day-hikers trek rarely traveled canyons of the Santa Rita Mountains, following a jeep trail along a perennial stream. The trail passes several abandoned mines, winds around rough-cut cliffs, and leads to waterfalls rushing off lichen-spotted rocks.

Photographer Randy Prentice and I parked at the junction of Forest Service roads 72 and 72A and began our 12-mile round-trip up the rutted track. Ambling along under a canopy of Fremont cottonwoods and Arizona sycamores, we marveled at the pristine beauty of the riparian vegetation. The jeep trail disappeared several times as it merged with the streambed, encouraging fancy footwork as we jumped from rock to rock.

Silvery blue and lemon yellow butterflies fluttered against purple Tahoka daisies and the fluted scarlet flowers of the golden-beard penstemons. Patches of yellow tail-leaf pericome drew large striped bumblebees, oblivious to the flowers' distinctive odor (early Spaniards called it *yerba de chivato*, or "the herb of the he-goat" for its smell).

Knowing how close we were to Madera Canyon, the world-renowned birders' paradise, I searched the skies for warblers, tanagers, and hummingbirds, just some of more than 300 species that abound in the area. Signs at the trailhead mentioned vermilion flycatchers and the elusive Strickland woodpeckers. We saw a vermilion flycatcher but no woodpeckers.

At 5,000 feet, after 3 miles of hiking through picturesque glades and past the blocked remains of the Ultimo, Philadelphia, and Little Joker mines, we reached a junction — a footpath continuing through Temporal Gulch branches left, heading west into the mountains. We stayed on the jeep trail as it roamed northwest, crossing the clear stream several times before coming to a dead end at Wildcat Mine, a perfect spot for a rest and a snack. (The Arizona Trail segment mentioned further on takes off from that same junction, only it follows FR 72 north into the foothills.) — *Carrie M. Miner*

left: Nearby Madera Canyon commands the grander reputation with bird-watchers, but watchful hikers along Temporal Gulch may still spot a vermilion flycatcher. ROBERT CAMPBELL **opposite page:** Oak and black willow trees line Temporal Gulch's stony banks, with Josephine Peak rising in the background. RANDY PRENTICE

- ■ **How To Get There:** This hike is 201 miles south of Phoenix; 91 miles south of Tucson; and 5 miles north of Patagonia. From Patagonia, drive north on First Avenue from State Route 82. After 2.5 miles, the road enters the Coronado National Forest and becomes Forest Service Road 72, a dirt road passable by most passenger vehicles, which descends into Temporal Gulch. Park at the intersection of FR 72A and continue up FR 72 along Temporal Gulch on foot.
- ■ **Elevation:** 4,050 to 5,000 feet.

below: Barrel and saguaro cacti and scarlet-bloomed ocotillo edge the climb up Picketpost Mountain.
BERNADETTE HEATH
opposite page: A spiky agave cooly contrasts with the sunset colors lighting Picketpost's summit.
BERNADETTE HEATH

■ **Mileage:** 12 miles round trip.
■ **Seasons:** Spring, fall, and winter.
■ **Maps:** USGS Helvetia, Mount Wrightson, and Patagonia quadrangles; Forest Service map of Coronado National Forest.
■ **Nearest Supply Point:** Patagonia.
■ **Backcountry Information:** The start of this hike includes a segment of the Arizona Trail. From the border with Mexico to the state line with Utah, the Arizona Trail extends the length of Arizona through a cooperative system of interconnecting trails, or passages. Although not finalized at the time of this printing, the Arizona Trail is well on its way to completion.

Picketpost Mountain

On top of Picketpost Mountain, elevation 4,375 feet, stands a little red mailbox. Its perky flag urges visitors to "Sign in please" at the trail register, and they usually do. Their comments date back more than 12 years, each a token of someone's personal journey.

The little red mailbox also tells a story of its own, with these words etched into its door: "Resided for years at 98264. Once barreled over by a green John Deere tractor. . . . Repaired and replaced. . . . Nearly destroyed by a white Chev 1978 sedan. . . . Retired, reshaped, and relocated this spot. . . . Believed to be relatively safe."

Clunky and squarish, Picketpost resembles a huge, flat-topped iceberg carved from the cliffs of nearby Apache Leap. This "berg," however, looms more than 1,700 feet above the desert near Superior, about 60 miles east of Phoenix. Its summit encompasses enough flat space to hold two football fields.

The mountain earned its name during the 1870s when it served as a lookout post (called a "picket") for Gen. George Stoneman's infantry headquartered at nearby Camp Pinal.

The trek to the top — a combination hike and scramble — presents a challenge. Though it is reached by several different "routes," none qualifies as an official trail.

The most popular track takes hikers directly up the west face. It starts south of

U.S. Route 60 and follows a dirt-road section of the Arizona Trail south for about a quarter of a mile before heading southeasterly up an abandoned mine road toward the mountain's western midsection. From there, a variety of paths converge in a shadowed notch that allows scramblers a passage to the top. Each variation on this route features either treacherous gravel, polished slick-rock, trickling waterfalls, large chockstones, or all of the above, making it a stimulating test for the strong and agile.

Two of the strongest, most agile climbers at Picketpost over the years have been Len Coons and Fred Eichinger, both former winter residents of nearby Superior.

Coons and Eichinger spent a lot of time maintaining routes and scaling their beloved mountain. During January 1995, one or the other signed the summit register seven times over 16 days, once recording an ascent time of 1 hour, 15 minutes. Such speed and durability would be a feat for any healthy 20-year-old, but these men were past 70 then.

Most hikers take 2 hours or more to reach the top. There, they stroll around and take in the startlingly clear views of the Superstition Mountains, Four Peaks, the Santa Catalina Mountains, Picacho Peak, and the Sierra Anchas. — *Rick Heffernon*

- **How to Get There:** From Phoenix, take U.S. Route 60 east to Forest Service Road 231 at approximately .4 of a mile east of Milepost 221 (5 miles west of Superior). Turn south and proceed for about .3 of a mile to a "T" intersection with an old paved road. Turn east and continue .6 of a mile to a parking area at the Arizona Trail's Picketpost Mountain trailhead. (While a Forest Service trailhead is the starting point, this is not an official trail; you'll see that some hikers have established their own use trail.)
- **Elevation:** About 2,675 feet at the start; about 4,375 feet at the summit.
- **Mileage:** 2 miles, roughly, one way.
- **Seasons:** November to April.
- **Maps:** USGS Picketpost Mountain quadrangle; Tonto National Forest map of the Superstition Wilderness.
- **Nearest Supply Points:** Superior, Globe.
- **Backcountry Information:** Carry water. As an unofficial use trail, this route is not maintained by the Forest Service. Some scrambling and route-finding ability is a must. The Picketpost Mountain/Reavis Canyon passage of the Arizona Trail connects with this trail early on before heading in a different direction.

Agua Caliente Wash

Take sturdy legs and both your lungs for this very steep trail.

At the trailhead, between Elephant Head and Mount Hopkins, about 45 miles southeast of Tucson, a sign says Agua Caliente Saddle is a 1.7-mile hike, but a guidebook said 2.2 miles. That seemed more accurate when we hiked it. In that short distance, you climb a little more than 2,600 feet.

From the trailhead, the first half mile seems easy: a little up, a little down, but

above: Just a touch of white on a rock outcropping pinpoints the Smithsonian Institution's Whipple Observatory, which overlooks Agua Caliente Trail from atop Mount Hopkins.
DAVID ELMS, JR.

generally a pleasant walk through clearings in the boulders and oak trees parallelling Agua Caliente Wash, which carries water most of the year. The trail later crisscrosses the wash several times. A half mile up the narrow canyon, the trail enters Mount Wrightson Wilderness and becomes a series of short, steep switchbacks.

Shortly before the steepest ascent — just below the saddle — are three open mine shafts, deep, dangerous, and flooded. Heed the posted warnings.

Beyond, the trail becomes nearly vertical in places before reaching a small saddle at 7,260 feet. You'll see Mount Wrightson to the east.

From Tucson, take Interstate 19 south to Canoa Road (Exit 56). Go left under the highway and turn right onto the frontage road to Elephant Head Road (signs direct you). After 3 miles, turn left onto Elephant Head Road. Cross the Santa Cruz River and watch for Mount Hopkins Road about a half mile up on your right. Turn right and drive 5.5 paved miles (Forest Service Road 184) to FR 183. You'll see a sign for "Agua Caliente Canyon" and another that says "Primitive Road." Turn left. The primitive dirt road requires a high-clearance vehicle, but not four-wheel drive. Drive 2.5 miles to a dirt road that makes a sharp left. The sign says "Dead End 2 miles." Turn left onto that road for .7 of a mile. Park in the clearing on the left and look for the stenciled steel trail sign on the right.

You can buy a wilderness map from the Coronado National Forest or carry the Mount Wrightson and Mount Hopkins USGS quadrangle maps. — *Sam Negri*

Cherum Peak Trail

Up little-known Cherum (pronouned "shrum") Peak Trail I climb, past scrub oak and piñon pine to the 6,983-foot summit and the marvelous view.

Through invigorating clean air, I can see for more than a hundred miles in any direction. The jagged line of the Colorado River fault 25 miles away seems much closer. Big valleys stretch out below, and volcano cones near Williams clear the horizon 90 miles to the east. Kingman is 20 miles south and mostly out of sight. But I look directly down upon the onetime silver town of Chloride, now busily mining tourists.

Cherum Peak is the second highest point in the Cerbat Mountains, a range picked and probed by miners for more than a century. The 2-mile-long Cherum Peak Trail can be climbed easily but stops just short of the summit. A slightly lower overlook offers a good view just past the second stock gate, but watch out for the unfenced mine shaft nearby.

Cherum Peak Trail was officially opened in August 1994. The Mohave County Trails Association surveyed the route, and local hikers helped carve the trail. Only a few people had signed the register when I first passed that way, three days after an October snowfall. Patches of snow still clung to shaded clefts. A runt-size mule deer, judging from its small tracks, had climbed the trail partway to reach the state-managed game water troughs at the base of Cherum Peak.

Consider the drive up to the trailhead as part of the adventure. I had no difficulty reaching the trailhead in a sedan, although the graded road climbs steeply, creeps around jackknife corners, and hangs out for 2 miles along a mountainside offering an unobstructed view of a 2,000-foot plunge to the outskirts of Chloride. For maps, you may want to take BLM's Davis Dam topographical map or the USGS Chloride quadrangle.

To reach the Cherum Peak trailhead from Kingman, drive 20 miles north on U.S. 93 to the Big Wash Road turnoff. The turnoff, about 1 mile beyond the Chloride turnoff, is marked by a BLM sign. High-clearance vehicles are recommended. — *Bob Thomas*

below: Once inside Pico del Aguila Ventana, or Eagle's Beak Arch, hikers have a fine view of the surrounding volcanic terrain.
PATRICK FISCHER

opposite page: From Cherum Peak Trail in the Cerbat Mountains, you can see the plateau country near the Grand Canyon.
GEORGE STOCKING

Eagle's Beak Arch

The great hole in the mountain above me grew ever larger as I drove over the twisting up-and-down road studded with lava rocks.

My goal was a geologic feature near the top of a rugged volcanic peak, part of the Harquahala Mountain range, which overlooks the small community of Aguila 85 miles northwest of Phoenix.

This natural ventana, or "window," — about 50 feet wide and 30 feet high — has a rounded rock formation above the opening that looks just like the curving beak of a giant predatory bird. Spanish-speaking settlers called it *Pico del Aguila Ventana*, or "Eagle's Beak Window." It's also called Eagle's Beak Arch.

On this late fall visit, the sun made the dark red rocks hot to the touch.

The window was about a thousand feet above me, and I decided to take the shortest route, straight up the steepest, rockiest pitch.

The terrain doesn't offer much of a choice. There's no path; just a very steep climb with a lot of loose rocks, catclaw, and cacti. Weaving through the thorny brush and lava rocks can be a hands-and-knees experience at times. But there are no big cliffs to climb, just a couple of 20- or 30-foot-high ledges that must be crossed. A reasonably fit person should be able to reach the window inside of an hour.

Approaching the southern side of Pico del Aguila, you have the best view of the great beak.

Pico del Aguila is 4 miles south of Aguila on the upper saddle between Eagle Eye Mountain and Eagle Eye Peak. Take paved Eagle Eye Road south (you can see the eagle beak formation from the road) and drive through a pass to an electrical power transmission line. Cross the dip in the road under the line and immediately turn left onto a dirt road and then turn left again within the first 50 feet. Follow this road for 1.5 miles as it twists and turns north. The road crosses and recrosses a dry wash. After the third crossing, take the left fork and climb up the two-track road to the pass underneath the window. You climb to the window from here. Several dirt tracks lead from the transmission line toward the window, but they're badly eroded. Stay on the one described. — *Bob Thomas*

Kendrick Peak

At 10,418 feet, Kendrick Peak is more than 2,000 feet lower than the crest of the San Francisco Peaks; however, unlike the San Francisco Peaks, Kendrick Peak offers an unrestricted 360-degree panorama from its summit. Kendrick thrusts itself out of the 7,000-foot-high Coconino Plateau more than 3,000 feet, providing the greatest vertical relief in the southern half of the Kaibab National Forest.

While the 4-mile climb to the summit is an invigorating hike, it's the destination, not so much the journey, that is your reward. As early as 1902, cartographer Francois Mathes used Kendrick as his key triangulation point for the first topographic map of the Grand Canyon, and with good reason. From the summit of this natural lookout you can clearly see the Grand Canyon to the north, the Little Colorado River gorge to the northeast, and the San Francisco Peaks to the east. Looking in any other direction, you'll need a good set of maps to identify all the other mountain ranges.

To reach Kendrick Peak, drive northwest from Flagstaff on U.S. Route 180 for 17 miles to Forest Service Road 193. Turn west on FR 193 and drive 4.5 miles to FR 171. Take FR 171 for 3 miles to FR 171A. Turn right and FR 171A will dead-end at the Kendrick Peak trailhead a mile farther.

Picacho Peak State Park

Thrusting out of a broad desert plain, the jagged, black peak can be seen 60 miles away. It beckons to be climbed. At the west end of the Picacho Mountains and 40 miles north of Tucson just off Interstate 10, Picacho Peak is a striking landmark. It is often mistaken for a volcanic neck. It is mostly volcanic rock, but from the type of lava

opposite page:
Picacho's summit of eroded, tilted lava flows is a prominent landmark for people driving Interstate 10 between Tucson and Phoenix.
TOM DANIELSEN

that becomes plastered onto the flanks of a volcano, not the magma that cools within the neck. The layers have been tilted on end, and erosion has sculpted the material into a prominent peak.

Hunter Trail climbs 1,500 feet in 2.2 miles to the summit. If you are not psyched for a rigorous climb, stroll along the .5-mile Calloway Trail at the base of the peak. Picacho Peak is well known for dazzling displays of desert wildflowers in the spring. There is a day-use fee.

above: Ocotillo, saguaro cactus, and wildflowers trim a hillside in Picacho Peak State Park.
DAVID H. SMITH

Woodchute Trail

From Prescott, take U.S. Route 89A east across the pass on Mingus Mountain to Potato Patch Campground. Then take Forest Service Road 107 to Powerline Tank. Woodchute trailhead is a few hundred yards beyond the pond.

It's 2 miles from Powerline Tank to Woodchute Tank, and another mile to the summit for some great views of the Verde Valley, Sedona's famous red rock country, Sycamore Canyon Wilderness, San Francisco Peaks, Kendrick Peak, and Bill Williams Mountain. There is an 800-foot elevation change from the Woodchute trailhead, at about 7,000 feet, to the top of Woodchute Mountain.

Once upon a time, a giant wooden trough brought logs splashing down the mountain. They were used in the copper mines of Jerome, which is about 5 miles beyond Potato Patch. Today Jerome is Arizona's liveliest "ghost" town.

When You Go

Bull Pasture
www.nps.gov/orpi/
Organ Pipe Cactus National Monument
(520) 387-6849
Entry fee, backcountry camping permit.
Camping fee. Food, services, lodging in Ajo.

Palm Canyon Trail
southwest.fws.gov/refuges/arizona/kofa.html
Kofa Wildlife Refuge Headquarters
356 West 1st Street, Yuma, AZ;
(928) 783-7861
Camping. No drinking water or rest rooms.

Arizona State Parks
www.pr.state.az.us/parklist.html
Arizona State Parks Department,
(602) 542-4174.

Picacho Peak State Park
(520) 466-3183
Entry fee. Camping. Visitor center.

Oak Creek
www.fs.fed.us/r3/coconino/rec_redrock.html
Coconino National Forest, Supervisor's Office,
2323 East Greenlaw Lane, Flagstaff, AZ;
(928) 527-3600.

Sedona Ranger District
(928) 282-4119
Call for directions, regulations, fees, Red Rock
Pass for parking (see Chapter 7).

Kendrick Peak
www.fs.fed.us/r3/kai/recreation/trwc.html
Kaibab National Forest, Supervisor's Office,
800 South 6th Street, Williams, AZ;
(928) 635-8200.

Williams/Forest Service Visitor Center
200 West Railroad Avenue, Williams, AZ
(800) 863-0546 (also TTY)
(928) 635-4707 or 4061 (also TTY)
Cooperative visitor center open 8 A.M. to 5 P.M.
daily, weekends. Maps, information, exhibits.

Williams Ranger District
(928) 635-5600
Call for information on recreation, directions,
regulations, fees.

Cathedral Wash
www.nps.gov/glca/lferry.htm
Glen Canyon Recreation Area, Headquarters
(928) 608-6200

24-Hour Emergency, (800) 582-4351

Carl Hayden Visitor Center, U.S. 89, Page, AZ
(928) 608-6404
Daily, 8 a.m. to 5 p.m.; Memorial Day to
Labor Day, 7 a.m. to 7 p.m.

Lees Ferry Ranger Station, (928) 355-2234

Navajo Bridge Interpretive Center,
U.S. 89A near Lees Ferry
Daily, mid-April to October; weekends only,
early April and November.

Temporal Gulch and Agua Caliente Trail
www.fs.fed.us/r3/coronado/nrd/nogo.htm
Coronado National Forest, Supervisor's Office
300 West Congress Street, Tucson, AZ;
(520) 670-4552.

Nogales Ranger District
(520) 281-2296
Call for seasonal restrictions, regulations,
use fees.

Picketpost Mountain
www.fs.fed.us/r3/tonto/districts/globe/globe.htm
Tonto National Forest, Supervisor's Office
2324 East McDowell Road, Phoenix, AZ;
(602) 225-5200
(602) 225-5395 — TTY

Globe Ranger District
(928) 402-6200
Call for seasonal restrictions, regulations,
use fees.

Woodchute Trail
www.fs.fed.us/r3/prescott/
Prescott National Forest, Supervisor's Office
344 South Cortez Street, Prescott, AZ;
(928) 771-4700; TTY/TDD, (928) 771-4708.

Chino Valley Ranger District
(928) 636-2302
(928) 636-3108 — TTY/TDD
Call for directions, regulations, fees.
Potato Patch Campground (fee).

Cherum Peak Trail and Eagles' Beak Arch
Bureau of Land Management (BLM), Arizona
State Office, 222 North Central Avenue, Phoenix,
AZ; (602) 417-9200.

Kingman Field Office (Cherum Peak)
www.az.blm.gov/kfo/index.htm
(928) 692-4400

Phoenix Field Office (Eagle's Beak Arch)
www.az.blm.gov/pfo/index.html
(623) 580-5500

5 grand canyon hikes

Galen Snell was a soft-spoken country boy from Kansas. My psychology professor at Scottsdale Community College, he'd been inviting me to hike down the Boucher Trail in the Grand Canyon. Why bother, I'd thought. I'd been backpacking in the Superstition Mountains since my early teens, and they represented everything that was wild about Arizona.

Galen pressed on, subtly, and by semester's end, I relented.

We were walking along the enchilada-red Hermit formation when it hit me. Here we were hiking one of the airiest stretches of trail I'd ever been on, and it felt like I could fly. The Colorado River was at our feet, thousands of feet below; the North Rim felt like I could just reach out with my right hand and grab a handful of ponderosas. East or west as far as you could see, upcanyon and down, awesome tributary canyons drained into the Colorado River — 70-some canyons in all, Galen said.

That hike taught me Arizona was more than my Superstition Mountains.

Whole guidebooks have been published about hiking the Grand Canyon. This chapter is just a quick sampling of some of the many hikes available to hikers, whether they're novices or experts. If you want to enjoy the beauties of the Grand Canyon, you'll have many choices to select from besides just strenuous backpacking expeditions.

On a warm day early in the summer of 1540, three Spanish soldiers tried to reach the bottom of the Grand Canyon. General Francisco Vasquez de Coronado, camped near present-day Zuni, New Mexico, had heard of a gorge far to the west. He thought perhaps it might be part of a fabled waterway across North America. He sent a small detachment to explore it.

The diary of Pedro de Castañeda, another soldier, reveals that they succumbed

to a common illusion that distances are shorter than they seem. The Spaniards would not believe that the Canyon was as deep, or the Colorado River as wide, as their Hopi guides claimed. They returned exhausted late in the afternoon, having climbed perhaps one-third of the way into the Canyon.

Hiking the Canyon is not nearly that demanding today (although it can be if you prefer). Some of the well-maintained trails are like boulevards compared to hiking elsewhere in Arizona. Yet hiking in the Canyon is the ultimate outdoor experience for many. Just be sure to go prepared. Morning temperatures are brisk at the South Rim, 6,876 feet elevation, and the North Rim at 8,200 feet. But summer midday temperatures of 110° F. are common at the Canyon's floor.

For the very same reasons Grand Canyon is so awesome, we cannot adequately summarize in this chapter all the potential human experiences it offers. Numerous books and trail guides are available to enhance your future adventures in the grandfather of all canyons.

A fine rim-to-rim hike starts on the North Rim (preferably) and ends at the South Rim. If you hike north-to-south, it is best to emerge via Bright Angel Trail. If you begin at the South Rim, you will find South Kaibab a shorter but steeper way to enter the Canyon than Bright Angel. — *John Annerino*

Bright Angel Trail

It is easy to be lured down, down, down the Bright Angel Trail with no intention of going all the way to that tiny silver strand of water below — actually the roaring Colorado River. Yet many hikers, particularly summer tourists, unexpectedly find themselves at the bottom, facing the climb back out. Hikers need to be aware that they face the equivalent of hiking a mile-high mountain, in reverse, and prepare accordingly. You need food, water, proper clothing, and footwear. If you go properly prepared, the greatest danger is being stunned by the Canyon's grandeur.

Havasupai Indians, and prehistoric people before them, followed the same route to reach their gardens near what is now Indian Garden on a plateau midway to the canyon bottom. In more modern times, miners developed the trail to reach mines in the Canyon. It was named the Cameron Trail for Ralph R. Cameron, one of the mine owners. When Cameron realized there was more money in tourists than in minerals, the Cameron Trail became a toll road. The wily entrepreneur charged Canyon visitors $1 each to use it.

The Santa Fe Railroad, which wanted a piece of the tourist action, challenged Cameron's claims, which were invalidated about 1920. The trail became the property of Coconino County, which in turn traded it to the federal government in 1928. In 1937 the U.S. Board of Geographic Names named the route Bright Angel Trail.

Major John Wesley Powell, who explored the Colorado River in wooden boats in 1869 and 1872, first applied the name to Bright Angel Creek, which enters the Colorado from the north. The name spread. In fact, the trailhead is a short walk west of Bright Angel Lodge at the South Rim.

The 9.5-mile trail is plainly marked and impossible to mistake. It leads down through thick layers of Kaibab limestone and Coconino sandstone. The Civilian Conservation Corps of the 1930s built the rest houses which still serve 1.5 and 3 miles down the trail. At a switchback called Two-Mile Corner, pictographs date back to A.D. 1300, showing how long the trail's natural course has been followed. Any of these three points would be a likely destination for a short hike.

Switchbacks called Jacob's Ladder lead down through the 500-foot-thick layers of a formation called Redwall limestone. Indian Garden is a welcome refuge to hikers going up or down the trail. It is 4.7 miles from the trailhead, and its towering cotton-

wood trees are visible from several areas. There is a ranger station here, corrals, a developed campground, water, and toilets. It makes a good turnaround point for a one-day hike from the South Rim. This also is the beginning of the relatively flat, 1.5-mile trail out to the end of Plateau Point, which offers gorgeous views of the Inner Gorge.

After Bright Angel leaves Indian Garden, it descends through Tapeats Narrows and then into the Devil's Corkscrew, winding hairpins of trail through the Vishnu schist, some of the earth's older rocks. The trail bottoms out along the bed of Pipe Creek. At Pipe Creek rest house near the Colorado River, you pick up River Trail and follow it east 1.7 miles to the suspension bridge leading to Bright Angel Campground and Phantom Ranch on the north side of the river. Continue straight on River Trail, and you reach the foot of South Kaibab Trail; the old suspension bridge is a mile farther east. — *John Annerino*

above: A shady ramada at Indian Garden Campground, 4.5 miles below the South Rim, offers shelter for a midday picnic.
RICHARD L. DANLEY

- **How To Get There:** To reach the South Rim from Flagstaff, go 81 miles north on U.S. Route 180; from Williams, go north 28 miles on State Route 64 to U.S. 180 and take it north 31 miles. Bright Angel Lodge in the Grand Canyon Village is a short drive beyond the park entrance; the Bright Angel trailhead lies near the lodge.
- **Primary Access:** South Rim, and River Trail from Phantom Ranch.
- **Elevation:** 6,876 to 2,400 feet.
- **Mileage:** 9.5 miles to Bright Angel Campground.
- **Escape Points:** South Rim, Indian Garden, or Phantom Ranch by trail.
- **Seasons:** Fall through spring are best; summer can be hot.
- **Maps:** USGS Grand Canyon, Phantom Ranch, and Bright Angel Point quadrangles.
- **Nearest Supply Points:** Tusayan, Flagstaff, Williams, and Cameron.
- **Backcountry Information:** Permits are required for all overnight hiking. No fires are permitted. Contact the park's backcountry reservations office.

North Kaibab Trail

To reach the head of the North Rim's modern North Kaibab Trail, drive 2 miles north of Grand Canyon Lodge. The trailhead parking lot is on the right (east) side of State Route 67. Like Bright Angel over on the South Rim, the North Kaibab Trail is easy to follow all the way to the river. The only difficulties you may encounter, aside from length and steepness, are rock slides that occasionally cover upper sections of the trail during spring thaw or after a summer squall.

The steepest section of the North Kaibab Trail, the 4.7-mile stretch from the trailhead down Roaring Springs Canyon to its confluence with Bright Angel Canyon, drops some 3,400 vertical feet. En route to the confluence, you'll pass Roaring Springs day-use area on the right. Nearby buildings, occupied and maintained by Park Service personnel who operate the Roaring Springs pumphouse, send water to both rims.

From this confluence it's another 2 miles down Bright Angel Creek to Cottonwood Campground and its seasonally manned ranger station. A mile farther, you'll reach Ribbon Falls Trail junction. The non-maintained trail to Ribbon Falls is marked by cairns, as is its fording of Bright Angel Creek. (You may also use the bridge .5 mile north of the fording.)

It is another 6 miles down Bright Angel Creek to the Phantom Ranch-Bright Angel Campground area.

below: A verdant microclimate exists at the base of 150-foot-tall Ribbon Falls, just off the North Kaibab Trail near Cottonwood Campground.
RICHARD L. DANLEY

If you're planning a rim-to-rim hike from the North Rim to the South Rim — and you will find it easier hiking north to south — consider coming out on the Bright Angel Trail; it's a few miles longer than the South Kaibab, but it's not as steep, so your legs will have more of a chance to recover. Besides, there's water on the Bright Angel, and there isn't any on the South Kaibab. — *James E. Cook*

above: From this bridge on the North Kaibab Trail, hikers gain an almost-aerial view of the Grand Canyon's depths. TOM BEAN

- **How To Get There:** To reach the North Rim, take U.S. Route 89 north from Flagstaff to Bitter Springs, then take U.S. 89A across the Colorado River to Jacob Lake, and go south 30 miles on State Route 67 to the park entrance; Grand Canyon Lodge and the Rim itself are another 14 miles in.
- **Primary Access:** North Kaibab trailhead, Old Kaibab Trail, Bright Angel Trail, South Kaibab Trail.
- **Elevation:** 8,241 feet at trailhead to 2,400 feet at Colorado River.
- **Mileage:** 14 miles one way.
- **Seasons:** June through September from North Rim, all year from South Rim — but expect snow, ice, rock falls, and harsh conditions above Roaring Springs during winter.
- **Maps:** USGS Bright Angel Point quadrangle.
- **Nearest Supply Points:** Fredonia, Page, Vermilion Cliffs, Jacob Lake, North Rim, Grand Canyon Village.
- **Backcountry Information:** Contact the Grand Canyon's backcountry office. Permits are required for all overnight hiking. No fires permitted.

Havasu Canyon

Located in a remote area at the western end of the Grand Canyon, Havasu Canyon has high waterfalls, turquoise-colored pools, and beautiful scenery. It is a strenuous 10-mile hike down from the parking area at Hualapai Hilltop, on the Hualapai Reservation, to the campground. Although you can hike in and out in two days, allow three or four days to enjoy the waterfalls and hike farther down the canyon. It is 9 beautiful, but difficult miles beyond the campground to the Colorado River. May through October is best.

This canyon is the home of the Havasupai Indians. Permits for hiking and camping must be acquired well in advance.

To get there, drive 55 miles northeast of Kingman on Old U.S. Route 66. Turn north on Indian Route 18, and, after 60 miles, you'll arrive at Hualapai Hilltop parking area and trailhead.

Transept Trail

I set off to hike the 1.5-mile Transept Trail on the Grand Canyon's North Rim, with the slightly haughty scorn of a veteran hiker: How could this pitifully short, virtually flat trail offer even a taste of the magnificent beauty I've found along the lengthy, demanding routes in the Grand Canyon?

Barely five minutes into the hike, my attitude transforms as I see scenery as expansive and captivating as any I've seen anywhere.

above: On the Hualapai Indian Reservation, dawn's light illuminates a bluff in Quartermaster Canyon, a side canyon at the Grand Canyon's western end.
JACK DYKINGA

opposite page: Vivid blue-green from natural minerals it dissolves from canyon rock formations, Havasu Creek wends through the lower end of Havasu Canyon, one of the Grand Canyon's extensive network of side canyons.
DAVID H. SMITH

The Transept Trail, which traces the Canyon's very lip as it wends from the North Rim Campground to Grand Canyon Lodge, is essentially one long vista point. From the safe vantage point of the wide, well-maintained trail, a hiker's biggest challenge is finding a way to take in the geologic masterwork without being overwhelmed by its sheer immensity.

My eye goes first to the dizzying depths of the Transept, a sheer-walled gorge plunging 3,000 feet below its namesake trail. Rocks of a hundred hues cut elegant forms and build to the climax of 8,052-foot Oza Butte, far across the Transept southwest of the trail.

The Transept is but one side canyon in a jumble of side canyons, buttes, towers, and plateaus. Each step along the trail offers a slightly different take on the eons-old big picture. When I can yank my gaze from the Canyon's mesmerizing depths, I appreciate that the trail's inside edge is bounded by ponderosa pines, aspens, and spruce. Where the trail cuts briefly into the woods, I take care not to trample violet-blue lupines, scarlet penstemons, and other wildflowers.

As I reach the "grand finale" overlook point near the lodge, evening shadows cloak the Transept while the last sunlight paints the Rimrocks red. Through the clear air, I make out slim white fingers of snow clinging to the San Francisco Peaks scores of miles to the south. — *Douglas Kreutz*

Rim Trail

The Grand Canyon's inner trails take three times the energy to hike up as they do to hike down. There is an easier way to see the Canyon.

From eight years of hiking and roaming about the Canyon, I chose the Rim Trail on the South Rim as my favorite retreat. I can set my own pace and sit and enjoy the elegant views. At 7,000 feet, it's cool in summer, and I love the scent of piñon and ponderosa trees. The trail is paved, and mules are prohibited.

Some Grand Canyon maps show the Rim Trail as an unnamed dashed line. Others call it the "West Rim Trail" and "East Rim Trail." The former ends at Powell Memorial, the latter at Yavapai Point Museum. It is less than 4 miles between them.

The only huff-and-puff incline along the entire Rim Trail is the Bright Angel Fault, just west of the mule corral, a fracture that is 180 feet higher on the west side than the east. To avoid it, during the summer season, you can take the shuttle to Powell Memorial and hike the trail in reverse.

Among the main features on the trail are Trail Views I and II, which let you see much of the Bright Angel Trail and hundreds of staggering views that have no names at all.

The trail stays open all year, but I prefer early spring and late fall. You can actually find a parking place near the Rim, the air is crisp, and there's no summer haze. Even at this elevation, the summer sun can be intense. Wear a hat and light cottons with long sleeves to protect your skin. In winter, dress for frigid temperatures, but take sun protection. — *James Tallon*

When You Go

Grand Canyon National Park
www.nps.gov/grca/
P.O. Box 129, Grand Canyon, AZ 86023;
(928) 638-7888 — Information
(928) 638-7875 — Backcountry Office
(928) 638-2125 — FAX for permits
Admission fee; backcountry fees.
The Backcountry Information Center is open daily for walk-in visitors, 8 A.M. to noon and 1 P.M. to 5 P.M.; staff answer information calls 1 P.M. to 5 P.M. weekdays, except federal holidays. Unless staying at Phantom Ranch, all overnight visitors to the inner canyon need a backcountry permit.

Permits not required for day hikes below the Rim. Upon arriving, check trail conditions at the Backcountry Office. When summer temperatures are extreme in the inner canyon, the park may limit trail access to early morning and evening; for restrictions and closures, (928) 638-7888 (press 1-3-1).

North Rim/Grand Canyon National Park
Park boundary is 30 miles south of Jacob Lake on State Route 67; the actual rim edge is another 14 miles south.

Services: Weather permitting, North Rim facilities are open May 15 through October 16; then (weather permitting), the park stays open for day use only during the fall (no services or overnight facilities). State 67 from Jacob Lake to the park closes with first major snow, re-opens in May. Seasonal services at Kaibab Lodge (18 miles north of the park on State 67) and Jacob Lake: restaurants, fuel, some auto supplies, groceries, camping supplies.

Lodging: Grand Canyon Lodge, Reservations, (303) 297-2757.
Kaibab Lodge: Open seasonally. (928) 638-2389.
Jacob Lake Inn: Open seasonally; 45 miles north of park boundary. (928) 643-7232.

Camping: North Rim Campground: Fee. Reservations, (800) 365-2267; or make online at http://reservations.nps.gov/.

Two Forest Service campgrounds: DeMotte Campground, 16 miles north of the park boundary; Jacob Lake Campground, 45 miles north of the park boundary. Summer only.

With some restrictions, the Forest Service allows dispersed camping in the national forest outside the park. Kaibab National Forest, North Kaibab Ranger District in Fredonia, (928) 643-7395; Kaibab Plateau Visitor Center in Jacob Lake, 8 A.M. to 5:30 P.M. daily, (928) 643-7298.

Kaibab Camper Village: Commercial campground .25 mile south of Jacob Lake on State 67. Hookups. Reservations, (928) 643-7804 in summer; (928) 526-0924 in winter.

South Rim/Grand Canyon National Park
On the South Rim, the park's facilities, including food and lodging, are open all year. The community of Tusayan, outside the park entrance, has food, supplies, gasoline, and lodging.

Lodging: The South Rim lodges and Phantom Ranch at the bottom of the Canyon need reservations, up to 23 months in advance; (303) 29PARKS or (928) 638-2631.

Camping: Mather Campground: Reservations required March through November; (800) 365-2267 or online reservations: http://reservations. nps.gov/
No reservations December through February.

Desert View Campground: No reservations. RV camp: Has 84 sites; hookups, showers, laundry. Near Mather Campground. Reservations, (800) 365-2267.

Havasu Canyon
Havasupai Tourist Enterprises
General Delivery, Supai, AZ 86435;
(928) 448-2141
Rest rooms, food, lodging, and camping available, but limited. Small tribal town of Supai has provisions flown in by helicopter (mail comes by mule). Lodging reserved months ahead; Havasupai Lodge, (928) 448-2111. Small local market has general provisions.

Looking at the anxious smiles of my backpacking students, I thought perhaps the rugged terrain and tumultuous history of the Superstition Mountains inspired a trickle of dread beneath the stirring excitement of this, our final hike. Counting my two assistants, we were 15 strong (which is the maximum group allowed). We had come to traverse one peak in the range that Pima Indians once named *Kakatak Tamai*, "Crooked-Top Mountain," now known as Superstition Mountain.

This was the last weekend outing of a month-long backpacking and wilderness survival course I'd been teaching at Scottsdale Community College. Already, this diverse crew of high school and college students, housewives, attorneys, nurses, and retirees had hiked up Chiricahua Peak, trekked down the Boucher Trail into the Grand Canyon, and made a winter-style ascent of 12,670-foot Humphreys Peak.

Superstition Mountain was the last hurdle I could throw at them before they went on to become explorers in their own right.

Overnight backpacking gives the Arizona hiker the chance to weave skeins of day hikes and remote outback forays into tapestries of exhilirating exertion. Are you ready for your next challenge? — *John Annerino*

opposite page:
An Arizona camper scans the night sky with her binoculars.
FRANK ZULLO

Aravaipa Canyon

It was quiet in Aravaipa Canyon, except for the soft, soothing voice of running water and the rustling leaves of magnificent cottonwood trees. Aravaipa Creek is one of the few perennial streams in the Southwest. The Tohono O'Odham call it

A A-Ly Wai-Pi-A for "Little Wells," and the Apache call it "Little Running Water."

High-walled Aravaipa Canyon symbolizes primitive nature for many. It is so rugged that a Bureau of Land Management (BLM) brochure warns that it is "not a picnic ground." But a hiker who is in shape can walk through it handily, from one side of the Galiuro Mountains to the other. It is a tough environment, containing a fragile ecology.

The farther we hike into this streamside sanctuary, the more distant the sounds of civilization become. Soon they are washed away completely by the rustling cottonwoods and the water's almost placental tones.

The two of us have been hiking since morning, but not too early morning. There is no need for a daybreak attack when your day's objective is the other end of this 11-mile-long canyon. I'd invited Caroline Wilson along to identify and interpret the myriad species of flora and fauna in this lush canyon. As an interpretive specialist at Organ Pipe Cactus National Monument, she'd have the trained eye to spot the ash-throated flycatcher, the tiger rattlesnake, and the loach minnow.

As we wade beyond the knee-deep confluence of Booger Canyon, a golden eagle soars over the lip of the canyon wall a thousand feet above, carving long graceful arcs in the warm June sky.

So lush is Aravaipa's streamside (riparian) habitat that more than 300 wildlife species inhabit this small 6,699-acre wilderness — seven species of fish, eight of amphibians, 46 of reptiles, 46 of mammals, and more than 200 bird species. Those are just raw numbers, though. We're not taking into account what each of those critters eats, how long it lives, or how the presence of 3,000 to 4,000 hikers a year affects it.

We have sloshed and hiked almost 6 miles, and we have not seen one hiker yet. Not that I came out here to see other people, but the BLM office in Safford advised us that the daily quota of permits had all been spoken for.

In the fading late afternoon light, we see three barrel-thick cottonwood logs perched on a rock ledge 20 feet above the stream bed. They have been carried down and deposited there by a previous summer's flash flood.

Aravaipa Canyon drains a watershed on the east side of the Galiuros, cuts clean through the mountain range, and delivers the water to the San Pedro River. It has 14 major tributaries, four of them perennial, and drains an area of 541 square miles. That area includes the seldom-visited Galiuro Wilderness immediately to the south and part of 10,713-foot-high Mount Graham, the highest mountain in southern Arizona.

But we don't see, or hear, a soul. We have the place to ourselves, and that's fine by me. Sitting next to our small fire drying out wet tennis shoes, it's not hard to imagine how this canyon looked to the barefoot and sandal-clad Hohokam and Salado Indians; archaeologists believe they used Aravaipa Canyon as a primary migration route.

The next day, a mile short of our car, we see a family rafting down Aravaipa Creek. The creek at this point is maybe 24 feet wide and a foot or so deep. But mom, pop, and the kids are floating down Aravaipa Creek in inner tubes as if that's

opposite page: As inviting as Aravaipa Canyon seems, it poses a tough hike for those wanting to traverse it from one side of the Galiuro Mountains to the other. Aravaipa, protected by the federal Wilderness system, remains virtually unscarred by humans, yet people have lived in and near the canyon at least since the 19th century. DAVID MUENCH

the only way to see Aravaipa Canyon. Staring down at our prune-toed feet, and listening to the distant echoes of the family's laughter, I think we might have literally missed the boat on this one.

No matter how you try, you're not going to keep your feet dry. So avoid time-consuming detours to avoid getting them wet. If you're day hiking without a heavy pack, you can get by with tennis shoes and two pairs of socks. Some canyon hikers swear by a neoprene walking shoe called a Reefwalker. Take extra socks and a second pair of sneakers or thongs for camp.

If you're carrying a heavy pack, or if your ankles are prone to injury, wear high-top hiking boots. Although they'll get wet, they provide needed support for walking the rocky stream bed. Again take plenty of socks — wool socks make a difference in cool weather.

Because Aravaipa is such a short canyon, you have several options: Day hike from either entrance; backpack from either entrance for an overnight stay; or pack in and set up a base camp from where you can spend days exploring Aravaipa's tributary canyons: Parsons, Virgus, and Half-Acre canyons on the south side and Hell Hole, Paisano, Booger, Horse Camp, Javelina, and Painted Cave canyons on the north side. However you plan to hike the stem of Aravaipa Creek, the route is obvious: Stay in the creek bed, on dry ground when you can, and on faint pieces of trail

above: Cottonwoods and poplars, sporting their autumn colors along Aravaipa Creek, overwhelm a lone saguaro cactus.
DAVID MUENCH

when you find them. To be safe from flash floods during the wet seasons, always make a high camp; look for the "bathtub ring," or old high water line, and try to camp above it. — *John Annerino*

- **How To Get There:** To reach the west entrance, take State Route 177 south from Superior through Kearny, Hayden, and Winkelman. At Winkelman, turn south on State Route 77 for 11 miles to the Aravaipa Canyon Road. The turnoff is well marked, and the 13 miles of paved and gravel road which follow are suitable for passenger cars. To reach the east entrance, drive approximately 15 miles northwest of Safford on U.S. Route 70, then turn southwest on Klondyke Road. Follow Klondyke Road for approximately 45 miles to the entrance. Klondyke Road is a graded dirt road, maintained by Graham County and suitable for passenger cars.
- **Primary Access:** West entrance and east entrance. The east entrance is a longer drive, but is far prettier than the other.
- **Elevation:** East entrance, 3,060 feet. West entrance, 2,640 feet.
- **Seasons:** Springtime through fall; winter can be bone-cold unless your idea of a good time is hiking in a wet suit or hip waders. Summer can be hot; refreshing. The July/August monsoons can cause deadly flash floods.
- **Maps:** USGS Booger Canyon and Brandenburg Mountain quadrangles.
- **Nearest Supply Points:** Safford, Superior, Hayden, Winkelman, Oracle.
- **Backcountry Information:** Permits required (fee). Recommend requesting permits up to 13 weeks in advance. Small campfires permitted. Use driftwood and existing fire rings.

Humphreys Peak Trail

At daybreak, the three of us begin struggling along a perilously icy ridge 12,000 feet above sea level. We are weary from our rapid ascent. An arctic front has swept in from the west, and a fierce westerly wind has sent the chill factor well below zero. We are clawing our way up toward 12,356-foot Agassiz Peak, second highest mountain in Arizona, and we have voluntarily gone out of our way to try a winter ascent of a peak we can see only occasionally.

These delightful winter conditions are characteristic of alpine climbing. The San Francisco Peaks are the only Arizona mountains where climbers can "practice" before roaming the world for something more ambitious.

So we have come prepared for the extremes of both altitude and weather. We carry ice axes, crampons, lightweight stoves, down sleeping bags, and a mountain tent. We are wearing cumbersome layers of wool, down, and nylon. Yet if we do not force each other to keep moving — up or down — we could freeze to death.

I've been on the Peaks 40-odd times. Now I'm snowshoeing up the west flank of 12,633-foot Humphreys Peak with Randy Mulkey and Ken Akers. Both are experienced climbers, yet they'll take longer to adjust to the elevation because they live nearer sea level in Phoenix. Since I have the advantage of living and training

around 6,000 feet, I agree to break trail through the hip-deep powder snow. By the time we reach the tree line above 11,000 feet several hours later, my companions are beginning to feel the effects of mountain sickness: nausea, headache, general malaise. Mountaineers call it "going too high, too fast." So we heat a cup of mocha and wait for our lungs to catch up with our legs.

An hour later, we begin climbing a 45-degree slope, "front-pointing" with the tips of our crampons, in the icy snow. By sundown, our tent is pitched and we have wolfed down a dozen homemade tostadas, a jar of frozen jalapeño peppers, and a pound of Oreos.

Conditions deteriorate around midnight, and throughout the early morning hours it feels as though our tent will be blown off the mountain. Near dawn, Randy crawls outside and sees that the mile-long ridgeline leading to Humphreys Peak is being hammered by 30- to 40-mile-per-hour winds and heavy cloud cover. Over frozen ham sandwiches, we discuss our options: bash our way toward Humphreys and hope conditions improve; bail off the mountain; or make a dash for nearby Agassiz Peak.

The choice is obvious. We strike camp and agree to go for Agassiz as long as conditions don't further deteriorate into a whiteout. With every few yards gained, however, we are blown a step or two back, sometimes thrown to our knees. To compound matters, it is the first time I've ever seen overhanging cornices on this ridgeline. If we don't concentrate on where we put each step, the unstable snow could avalanche, hurtling us into the inner basin far below.

above: Caught in the odd half-light of moonrise over fresh snow on the San Francisco Peaks, autumn aspens stretch their pale trunks. DAVID MUENCH
opposite page: Two climbers make their way toward Humphreys Peak, with the Inner Basin behind them. TOM BEAN

When we reach the second highest summit of this sacred mountain an hour later, the icy cloud cover lifts long enough for us to see that we have just enough time to get off the mountain before the storm's full force hits us.

Climbing the Peaks is most frequently done during the fair summer months. While the Peaks are not technically difficult mountains to climb, the winds there are fickle: They can reach gale force, creating weather as unforgiving as any mountain range in the Southwest. So whether you day hike up to the summit, or plan on spending the night on the slopes, you must be conditioned for the altitude and be prepared for the sudden onset of extreme mountain weather. In winter, these mountains are no place for anyone but the most experienced with the best equipment. A winter ascent of the Agassiz or Humphreys summits is a marvelous adventure when you know what you're doing, but it's not for the everyday hiker or even for most so-called experienced hikers.

There are numerous approaches to take: any of the most obvious routes leading out of the Inner Basin; the old Waterline Trail paralleling White Horse Canyon up to Philomena Spring; the Weatherford Road, now a wilderness trail, which leaves 8,024-foot Schultz Pass and switchbacks up to the Agassiz-Humphreys ridgeline; or the Humphreys Peak Trail. Of these, the 4.5-mile-long Humphreys Peak

Trail is the most popular way to hike the Peaks. It's well-marked and easy to follow all the way to Agassiz-Humphreys ridgeline.

Hiking above the timberline is restricted to designated trails. Indiscriminate cross-country biking is prohibited in order to protect the fragile tundra habitat and, specifically, the San Francisco groundsel, a small endangered plant found only here. Summer hikes to Agassiz Peak are prohibited, but Humphreys Peak provides breathtaking views over the 18,200-acre Kachina Peaks Wilderness and the rest of northern Arizona — assuming a storm isn't in the offing. — *John Annerino*

- **How To Get There:** To reach Humphreys Peak trailhead, drive 5 miles north from Flagstaff on U.S. Route 180 to the turnoff for the Snow Bowl, then drive 8 miles up this steep mountain road to the upper lodge. That's where you pick up the trailhead.
- **Primary Access:** Humphreys Peak Trail and Weatherford Trail.
- **Elevation:** 9,500 feet at Humphreys Peak trailhead; 12,633 feet on Humphreys Peak.
- **Mileage:** 4.5 miles one way to Humphreys Peak.
- **Escape Routes:** Scree slope below Humphreys-Agassiz saddle down to lodge.
- **Seasons:** June through September is the most popular time. Beware of the summer monsoons, since you don't want to be anywhere on the Humphreys-Agassiz ridge line when lightning starts. During winter months, be prepared for severe alpine conditions.
- **Maps:** USGS Humphreys Peak quadrangle, although the newer Humphreys Peak Trail is not yet marked on it; Coconino National Forest map.
- **Nearest Supply Points:** Flagstaff, Williams.
- **Backcountry Information:** Permits are not required, but use the hiker's register near the trailhead. Camping and fires are not permitted above the tree line. Always check ahead with the forest office for changes and fire restrictions. If building a fire, use existing fire rings and wood that's dead and down. Use bikes on designated trails only.

opposite page: Many streams and drainages flow out of the Chiricahua Mountains, disguising the fact that the area essentially belongs to the Chihuahuan Desert. Branches from a big-tooth maple tree decorate the creek. JACK DYKINGA

Chiricahua Wilderness

The Chiricahua Mountains, a range of "sky islands" rising out of the flatlands in extreme southeastern Arizona, have a special place in the hearts of Arizonans, for their natural wonders and as ancestral home of the Chiricahua Apaches, the people of Cochise. The peaks rise more than 9,000 feet and harbor a diverse wealth of plants and animals.

This range has a maze of hiking trails, and the backbone of the system is the Chiricahua Crest Trail. On the north end of the mountains, you can reach the crest trail from Rustler Park via Pinery Canyon Road. For families and the not-so-gung-ho, Pinery Canyon Road provides a way of reaching the crest trail without the steep climb otherwise necessary. If you want less driving and more hiking, start at Morse Canyon trailhead at the end of West Turkey Creek Road.

Morse Canyon Trail climbs through ponderosa pine forest to a saddle near Johnson Peak, then follows a ridge east to Monte Vista Peak. Your dividend for this relatively steep 4-mile climb of 2,600 vertical feet is one of the best panoramas in

southeastern Arizona. Looking north, you can see Cochise Head rise above Chiricahua National Monument, and to the northwest the salt-crusted mud of Willcox Playa reflects the sun brightly.

In Pleistocene times, about 20,000 years ago, Sulphur Springs Valley held Lake Cochise. As the climate became hotter and drier, Lake Cochise shrank to Willcox Playa, where the sandhill cranes winter.

If you're hot and dry from your climb, Bear Springs is a refreshing water supply about half a mile down Monte Vista Peak's southwest flank.

Monte Vista Peak via Morse Canyon Trail is a good full-day hike. But we had three days, so we went stalking the wild iris. Between Chiricahua and Flys peaks, along the Crest Trail, lie two alpine meadows: Anita and Cima. Each is carpeted with Rocky Mountain iris — Western blue flag — and surrounded by stands of spruce and fir. Anita Springs and Booger Springs are dependable water sources. With most of the elevation gain under our belt, the crest trail was a casual walk through moss-covered firs and groves of aspen.

Just before reaching Anita Park, we heard a ruckus ahead. We were on alert for black bear, which I have often seen in the Chiricahuas, but it turned out to be three white-tailed deer browsing on young aspen. Black bears usually are not a problem, but overnight hikers should bag all food and scented items, then hang the bag by a

above: More obviously part of the arid Southwest, the grasslands bordering the Chiricahua Mountains abound with yucca and bear grass.
GEORGE H.H. HUEY

rope over a tree branch, at least 10 feet above the ground and 10 feet out from the trunk. Never take even candy or gum into your sleeping bag or tent.

It was early June, and the blue flag was just beginning to bloom. In Cima Park, I was saddened to see irises trampled by someone insensitive enough to camp in the middle of the meadow. There are excellent campsites just under the trees around the edge of the meadows, with the added comfort of a soft pad of pine needles.

From Round Park below Flys Peak, the Crest Trail runs about another 5 miles north to Barfoot Lookout on Buena Vista Peak. At the northern terminus of the Crest Trail, Barfoot Lookout provides a whole new, equally spectacular vista. With Monte Vista Lookout barely visible to the south, we were now 13.5 miles from the West Turkey Creek trailhead, so back we traveled; but at least it was mostly downhill.

There are 111 miles of developed trails in the Chiricahua Wilderness, and the Morse Canyon trailhead is only one of four main trailheads leading into backcountry. South to north, the other three are Rucker Lake, the south fork of Cave Creek, and Rustler Park. Once at the Morse Canyon trailhead, you can follow the well-marked, steep trail 2 miles to Johnson Saddle for a vigorous introductory hike. If you want to tackle a more ambitious day hike or an equally pleasant overnighter, it's another 2 miles to the lookout on Monte Vista Peak. The Chiricahua Crest Trail links Monte Vista Peak with Chiricahua Peak and its northern satellite, 9,666-foot Flys Peak. These 6.5 miles of trail are as fine as any in Arizona. So if you've driven this far, plan on spending another night in the Chiricahuas.

The best way to take in these three peaks might be for you to spend your first night atop Chiricahua Peak, day hike over to Flys Peak and back, pick up your pack, and spend your second night atop Monte Vista. That way you have a leisurely downhill stroll back to your car in the morning before tackling the drive back home. — *John Annerino*

- **How To Get There:** To reach the Morse Canyon trailhead from Tucson, drive 81 miles east on Interstate 10 to Willcox. Drive south from Willcox on State Routes 186/181, 43 miles to the turnoff for the West Turkey Creek Road, also known as Forest Service Road 41; it's 11 miles to the Morse Canyon trailhead.

  Pinery Canyon Road provides access to the Chiricahua high country trails and Coronado National Forest campgrounds. From its junction with State Route 181, just before the entrance to Chiricahua National Monument, Pinery Canyon Road climbs 16 miles to Onion Saddle. It is another 3 miles to Rustler Park at 8,400 feet. The graded gravel road is steep and winding, and no combination of vehicle and trailer over 41 feet long is permitted on the road. Snow can close the road in winter.

- **Primary Access:** Morse Canyon trailhead or Rustler Park.

- **Elevation:** 7,000 feet to 9,357 feet on Monte Vista Peak.

- **Mileage:** 4 miles one way from Morse Canyon to Monte Vista.

- **Escape Routes:** From Monte Vista Peak, back the way you came.

- **Seasons:** All year long. Summer is naturally the most popular time to seek relief from the heat in this cool refuge. Fall is incredibly colorful. Winter you may need cross-country skis.

- **Maps:** USGS Chiricahua Peak quadrangle. Coronado National Forest Douglas District recreation map.
- **Backcountry Information:** Permits are not required. Check with forest office for fire restrictions. Use existing fire rings and wood that's dead and down.

The Rattlesnake Fire in 1994 burned a patchwork pattern near the crest of the Chiricahua Mountains. However, much of the area was left untouched and still offers terrific hikes through spectacular scenery. A fire's aftermath presents hazards to watch for: loose boulders, falling trees and branches, and flash floods and mudslides when it rains. For safety, the Forest Service recommends: Stay on designated trails to minimize impact to burned forest floor. Camp in designated campgrounds and away from burned trees. Watch for flash floods in water courses during storms.

Paria Canyon

Rob Schultheis wrote in his book, *The Hidden Visit*: "Secret doors: there are so many of them out on the Colorado Plateau. Secret doors to other lost worlds, spinning their own time, turning on their own occult axes."

Buckskin Gulch was one such secret door. Through it, we had hoped to enter the heart of Paria (Pah-ree-uh) Canyon, a narrow sandstone defile which twists through a land every bit as sublime as the Grand Canyon. Buckskin at its best is a fissure carved through the soft sandstones of the Colorado Plateau by the relentless forces of erosion.

Rich Nebeker, Kimmie Johnson, and I were half an hour into our journey when Buckskin pinched together into a passageway no more than 2 feet wide. We squeezed through, holding our packs over our heads. Paria Canyon was used as an access route by Pueblo Indians and later by Mormon settlers traveling between northern Arizona and southern Utah. Its tributary of Buckskin seemed to be primarily a storm drain for spring runoff and summer flash floods. It was clogged with logjams and boulder slides that served as strainers for everything traveling through Buckskin, us included.

Now, that wouldn't be such a big deal if you could see where you were going. But with overhanging walls hundreds of feet high, there were few places that the sun could reach this labyrinth's gold and copper depths. When it did, it was as if we were walking through the incandescent glow of a light bulb. Otherwise, we either had filtered light to guide us from one shaft of light to the next or were walking in almost complete darkness.

We didn't think that was a major concern either, because we knew where one major drop-off occurred. But where the water pooled and formed stagnant ponds of quicksand, we thought about what the Spanish explorers Dominguez and Escalante said of the canyon country in 1776: *Salsipuedes.* Literally, "if you can." Get out if you can. Except for one, possibly two, places along its 15-mile course, there is no way out of Buckskin Gulch. You have the option of retreating the way you came, assuming a flash flood isn't thundering toward you, or continuing to probe your way downstream as if you were spelunking. Our course lay approximately 7.5 miles downstream from the Wire Pass trailhead where we knew we could climb out of the canyon, make camp, and assess the weather. But first we had to get there.

opposite page:
Three hikers make their way through Paria Canyon, a long slot in the floor of the Colorado Plateau as it extends into southern Utah. Floods wore away sandstone, leaving scallops and striations on this slot canyon's soaring walls. TOM BEAN

Our progress was barred by a Volkswagen-sized boulder. We voted to climb over it, because if the boulder did fall, we could ride it down — we thought. That was only slightly better than being caught underneath while crawling on hands and knees, in the growing darkness, through tangled logs and trees.

I removed my pack, stemmed the walls on both sides with hands and feet, and shimmied down until I could see how the footing looked. It looked clear.

I jumped, landing in the knee-deep muck. Quicksand, some call it. Having encountered this several times in the Paria Canyon "narrows," I knew the farthest I would sink would be up to my thighs.

This area is appropriately called the Cesspool. We slogged through this sucking, pudding-like substance in the twilight until we reached firmer ground. Our legs and feet were encased in a good half-inch of mud that was drying fast. Besides the isolated spots of quicksand, hiking this gulch typically means at least some wading through pools and mud.

When Kimmie looked up, she saw clouds, and we decided we should check the weather topside. It was the wrong season for rain, but flash floods are a danger at any time. It would be fatal to be flushed out of the canyon by a sudden storm. Finding a way up to a piñon-studded mesa on the north side of Buckskin, we discovered a view that took our breath away. We could see that Buckskin Gulch and Paria Canyon were but two canyons lost in a maze of reefs, buttes, and mesas.

Since this canyon maze is a drainage for Utah mountains much farther upstream, you won't be able to predict water levels in Buckskin and Paria. Give weather warnings serious heed, because changing weather can make unpaved access roads impassable and can scour the canyons with roaring flash floods.

Do not hike Paria Canyon and its tributaries during the summer storm season of July, August, and September. Winter is too cold and icy. Fall, late spring, and early summer are better times to hike, if you've checked available weather bulletins. For current forecasts, call the BLM offices in Kanab or St. George, Utah, and check the daily bulletins posted at the Paria contact station, Milepost 21 on U.S. Route 89 (about 30 miles west of Page).

There are several ways to hike the Paria Canyon area. The most popular is to start from the White House entrance and spend three or four days hiking the 38 miles downstream to Lees Ferry. In this primitive backcountry, there are no real trails and no signs, although the route is obvious once you're in Paria Canyon. Even in dry seasons, hikers must wade through ankle- to knee-deep water in many places. Appropriate footgear is essential.

Drinking water from Paria is safe if you purify and let it stand overnight to settle the heavy sediments.

Although the Paria River runs year-round, the last reliable spring is at Mile 25, about 13 miles above Lees Ferry. So bring large, collapsible containers to fill at the spring.

The second way to hike Paria is down Buckskin Gulch either via the Wire Pass trailhead or the Buckskin trailhead. Make this hike during a dry season. If you don't plan on hiking Buckskin Gulch to the Paria confluence in a single day, you'll want to camp on the rimrock above Buckskin. One certain place to get out of Buckskin is via the Middle Route located 6.4 miles below the confluence of Wire Pass and Buckskin Gulch. It's a bit of a scramble and can be hazardous.

Even in summer Buckskin Gulch can be chilly, so bring a jacket.

After the Cesspool 6.6 miles below the Wire Pass and Buckskin confluence, one other obstacle may impede your progress. A rock jam is located 3 miles below the Cesspool. It is accessible by steps chipped into the rock if you first lower your pack by rope, or you can scramble over the middle. The jam can be safely negotiated without much difficulty, but you may prefer to be belayed by your partner down the 12-foot descent with your own climbing rope.

Once you reach Buckskin's confluence with Paria Canyon, you either hike 31 miles through the length of Paria to Lees Ferry or complete a loop hike by hiking 6.8 miles up (north) to the White House trailhead.

Below the confluence with Bush Head Canyon, you can choose to follow an undeveloped trail through a boulder slide on the south side or continue walking in the Paria River bottom. Farther along, a well-beaten path often shortcuts the wide meanders. — *John Annerino*

- **How To Get There:** To enter Buckskin Gulch in Utah, take U.S. Route 89 32.5 miles west of Page, Arizona, to the House Rock Valley Road and turn south. The Buckskin Gulch trailhead is approximately 4.3 miles south of U.S. 89; the Wire Pass trailhead is 4 miles farther.

    To enter the White House trailhead for Paria Canyon, drive 28 miles west of Page on U.S. Route 89 to White House turnoff; turn left (south), and the trailhead is 1.8 miles beyond the turnoff.

    Due to flash flood danger, hike both Buckskin and Paria from top to bottom. However, if you are hiking all the way through Buckskin and Paria, you need to first park your shuttle vehicle at Lees Ferry. To reach the Lees Ferry trailhead, turn north off U.S. Route 89A at Marble Canyon and drive 6.5 miles to the parking area on the left side of the road. Some concessions may provide shuttle services for Paria Canyon hikers; check with the BLM offices in St. George and Kanab, Utah.

- **Primary Access:** Wire Pass, Buckskin Gulch, and White House trailheads. Do not try to hike Paria Canyon upstream from Lees Ferry due to flash flood danger.

- **Elevation:** White House, 4,400 feet; Buckskin Gulch, 5,500 feet; Wire Pass, 5,500 feet; Lees Ferry, 3,151 feet.

- **Mileage:** Wire Pass to Lees Ferry, 40.4 miles. Buckskin to Lees Ferry, 47.4 miles. White House to Lees Ferry, 38 miles.

- **Escape Route:** Back the way you came; via the Middle Route out of Buckskin; or the closest trailhead.

- **Seasons:** Fall, late spring, and early summer, but obviously avoid summer monsoons and heavy spring runoff.

- **Maps:** USGS Pine Hollow Canyon, West Clark Bench, Bridger Point, Glen Canyon City, Coyote Buttes, Wrather Arch, Water Pockets, Ferry Swale, and Lees Ferry quadrangles; BLM Paria Canyon biker's map.

- **Nearest Supply Points:** Kanab, Utah; Page and Marble Canyon-Vermilion Cliffs community (limited), Arizona.
- **Backcountry Information:** Day-use permits (fee) and overnight hiking reservation permits (fee) required. No campfires permitted. Overnight reservations available online.

Navajo National Monument

These prehistoric cliff dwellings mark the end of the Anasazi culture in northeastern Arizona. It is fascinating to stand in the stony silence of Betatakin or Keet Seel and speculate on what life must have been like 700 years ago.

Rangers lead a single daily tour to Betatakin, Memorial Day to Labor Day, on a first-come, first-served basis (25 tickets available per day). From the visitor center there is an elevation drop of 700 feet into the canyon. The strenuous round trip is 5 miles long and takes five hours.

Keet Seel is the largest cliff dwelling in Arizona. The arduous trail, at 16 miles round trip, makes a pleasant overnight backpack. It is open from Memorial Day to Labor Day. Permits are required for both hiking and overnight camping at Keet Seel. Reservations should be made two months in advance and then confirmed at least seven days before you visit to avoid cancellation. To get to Navajo National Monument, go 68 miles north of Flagstaff on U.S. Route 89. Turn east and go 62 miles on U.S. Route 160, then 10 miles north on Arizona Route 564.

Petrified Forest National Park and the Painted Desert

The Petrified Forest National Park and the Painted Desert beyond offer cross-country hiking and some outstanding overnight hikes in open terrain layered with fantasy colors. Around you spread low mesas, hummocks, and spires. Bring a polarizer for your camera if you have one.

In the park's northwest section, a trail leads into the Painted Desert. From Kachina Point, one can head across Lithodendron Wash north for about 2 miles to the Black Forest or 6 miles to Chinde Mesa.

You need a permit for all hiking and overnight stays off established trails. One can get lost easily in this maze of low hills and mesas, so pack your compass and topographic maps; the USGS Pilot Rock, Chinde Mesa, North Mill Well, Little Lithodendron Tank, Kachina Point, Pinta Point, Carrizo Butte, Adamana, Padilla Tank, and Agate House quadrangles cover the entire park (they don't note the Painted Desert, but refer to the Petrified Forest National Wilderness). Wilderness camping is allowed, but there are no campsites and no water or wood. For overnight stays, bring plenty of drinking water and a gas stove. Fall and spring are wonderful seasons to explore here.

Enter at the park's north entrance on Interstate 40, 25 miles northeast of Holbrook, or at its south entrance southeast of Holbrook on U.S. Route 180. The three visitor centers stay open all year: Painted Desert Visitor Center, at Interstate 40, 8 A.M. to 5 P.M.; Painted Desert Inn Visitors Center, 2 miles from the north entrance, 8 A.M. to 4 P.M.; and Rainbow Forest Museum, at the south entrance, 8 A.M. to 5 P.M. You can get the required overnight permit (no fee) at the Painted Desert Visitor Center or the Rainbow Forest Museum, but apply at least one hour before they close.

Arizona Trail

One man had a dream almost 30 years ago, and now it is close to coming true. Almost complete (portions are already open to adventurous hikers), the Arizona Trail is predicted to become one of the country's premier long-distance trails. The vision is that the Trail — ultimately a 790-mile non-motorized trail spanning Arizona from Mexico to Utah — will showcase the state's topographic, biologic, historic, and cultural diversity.

For Flagstaff teacher and avid hiker Dale Shewalter, the idea started brewing during the 1970s. He wanted to see a regional long-distance trail in Arizona. At one point, he actually backpacked a route through the state from Nogales to the Utah state line — in less than a month.

In other parts of the country, such backpacking trails like the Pacific Crest or Appalachian National Scenic trails may trace one mountain range. No single mountain range extends through Arizona, though, and the thrust of Shewalter's plan was to emphasize the state's ecological diversity.

Since he first proposed his concept to Arizona State Parks in the mid-1980s, the Trail's corridor has been developed with that specific emphasis, while linking public lands, mountain ranges, unique sites, and existing trails into one continuous route. Developing the corridor and bringing the plan to life has been the work of a partnership of several public agencies and the dedicated volunteers who form the Arizona Trail Association.

The Arizona Trail begins at the Coronado National Memorial on the U.S.-Mexico border and ends within the Bureau of Land Management's Arizona Strip District on the Utah state line. Between these two vividly separate points, the Trail's 18 major passages lead the adventurer through ruggedly spectacular scenery in six general areas: the Coronado National Memorial through the Huachuca Mountains, the Santa Rita Mountains to the Rincon Mountains, the Santa Catalina Mountains to the Mazatzal Mountains, the Mazatzal Mountains to the San Francisco Peaks, the San Francisco Peaks to the Grand Canyon, and the Grand Canyon to the Utah line.

As of early 2000, with 575 miles of the Trail now designated and signed, the public can explore almost all of the Trail's entire length. Mostly, the Arizona Trail uses existing trails and notes them by their original name and number. Since not every segment immediately connects with the next one, primitive roads temporarily link some trailheads; in those areas, new trail construction will be needed before the Trail can be called complete.

For the last several years, even in its rougher stages, the Arizona Trail has already been attracting hikers. For the interested backpacker, several books, pamphlets, and maps have been published to lend a helping hand.

When You Go

Petrified Forest and Painted Desert
www.nps.gov/pefo/
Petrified Forest National Park
(928) 524-6228
Entry fee, overnight backpacking permit (no fee). No campgrounds or lodging; nearby communities offer all services.

Chiricahua Wilderness
www.fs.fed.us/r3/coronado/douglas
Coronado National Forest, Supervisor's Office
300 West Congress Street, Tucson, AZ;
(520) 670-4552.

Douglas Ranger District
(520) 364-3468
Due to frequent drought, check on water availability, bears, campfire permits; also parking fees and overnight vehicle parking at trailhead parking areas.

Chiricahua National Monument
www.nps.gov/chir
(520) 824-3560
Entry fee.
Camping fees. No backcountry camping. Supplies, services, lodging in Willcox. Visitor center, campground fully accessible. Visitor center, 8 A.M. to 5 P.M., daily; closed Christmas Day.

Aravaipa Canyon
www.az.blm.gov/sfo/index.html
Bureau of Land Management (BLM),
Arizona State Office,
222 North Central Avenue, Phoenix, AZ;
(602) 417-9200.

Safford Field Office
(928) 348-4400
Permits, fees. Small parking lots at trailheads, plus primitive toilets, registration box, information board, self-serve fee station. You must sign in at registration box and pay fee (per person per day). No facilities. Check with BLM on camping locations.

Paria Canyon
http://paria.az.blm.gov
Bureau of Land Management (BLM) with Arizona Strip Interpretive Association (ASIA). Maps and services at interagency visitor center (St. George BLM office); open 7:45 A.M. to 5 P.M., weekdays; 9 A.M. to 5 P.M., Saturdays. (In season, Utah times are Mountain Daylight Time.)
(435) 688-3246.

Arizona Strip Field Office
345 E. Riverside Drive (off Interstate 15)
St. George, UT 84790
(435) 688-3200
(435) 688-3246 — Reservations
Day-use fee, overnight permit (fee). No campfires; pack out all trash and toilet paper. Also call BLM office in Kanab, Utah, (435) 644-4600.

Paria Information Station
30 miles west of Page on U.S. Route 89
open March 15 to November 15
8 A.M. to 5 P.M.
Water, rest rooms, maps, weather bulletins; no phone.

Keet Seel and Betatakin
www.nps.gov/nava/
Navajo National Monument
(928) 672-2700
No entrance fee, backcountry permit (no fee). Visitor center, 8 A.M. to 5 P.M., all year except Thanksgiving, Christmas, and New Year's days. Campground open all year, weather permitting. No hiking or backcountry travel on Navajo Nation land surrounding park.

Arizona Trail
www.pr.state.az.us/partnerships/aztrail/
aztrail.html
Crosses public lands managed by different agencies. Above Web page, on Arizona State Parks Web site, gives information on status, end points, elevations, land managers.

Arizona Public Lands Information Center
222 North Central Avenue, Phoenix, AZ
(602) 417-9300
Extremely useful resources; knowledgeable staff to assist you.

Arizona Trail Association
P.O. Box 36736, Phoenix, AZ 85067-6736
(602) 252-4794; http://aztrail.org/.
Nonprofit organization staffed by volunteers.

Area Code Note

Area codes in Arizona underwent several changes recently. First, the metropolitan Phoenix area was assigned three different area codes: (623) for the west metro area, (602) for Phoenix proper, and (480) for the east metro area.

In 2001, the area code for many Arizona communities outside of Phoenix changed from (520) to (928): Bullhead City, Camp Verde, Clifton, Cottonwood, Flagstaff, Gila Bend, Globe, Grand Canyon, Kingman, Lake Havasu City, Mohave Valley, Page, Parker, Payson, Pinetop, Prescott, Quartzsite, Safford, Sedona, Show Low, Somerton, Wickenburg, Window Rock, Winslow, and Yuma.

A small section of southern Arizona kept (520) as its area code: Ajo, Benson, Bisbee, Bowie, Casa Blanca, Casa Grande, Cascabel, Coolidge, Douglas, Elfrida, Eloy, Florence, Kayden, Komatke, Lone Butte, Maricopa, Nogales, Patagonia, Pearce, Portal, Sacaton, San Manuel, San Simon, Sasabe, Sells, Sierra Vista, Sunizona, Superior, Tombstone, Tucson, and Wilcox.

Red Rock Pass Program

The Forest Service now charges a recreational use fee for the Coconino National Forest lands in Sedona's red rock country. A vehicle parked on national forest land for non-commercial, recreational purposes must display a Red Rock Pass. If your vehicle isn't parked on forest property, then you won't need a pass, since the Forest Service emphasizes that this is not an entry fee. No pass is required for travel through red rock country nor for incidental activities that are part of driving through, such as stopping briefly to take a photograph or to use a rest room. If your vehicle does not display a valid pass in the windshield, you may be fined.

Red Rock Passes are sold at four Sedona-area visitor centers, operated jointly by the Forest Service, Sedona-Oak Creek Canyon Chamber of Commerce, Sedona Cultural Park, and the Arizona Natural History Association. You can buy a daily, weekly, annual, or grand annual pass; each

includes interpretive materials to enhance your awareness of this natural resource and a map of the trail network within red rock country. Each visitor center is there to help you with exhibits, brochures, conservation education services, and information on attractions, cultural events, recreational opportunities, and visitor amenities. For more information or to buy a pass online, go to: www.redrockcountry.org/.

North Gateway Visitor Center
(Arizona Natural History Association)
State Route 89A at Oak Creek Vista Overlook, at the top of Oak Creek Canyon.

West Gateway Visitor Center
(Sedona Cultural Park)
State 89A about 15 miles east of the town of Cottonwood.

Uptown Gateway Visitor Center
(Sedona-Oak Creek Chamber of Commerce)
State 89A at the Sedona-Oak Creek Chamber of Commerce in uptown Sedona.

South Gateway Visitor Center
(Coconino National Forest)
In Tequa 7000 on State 179 in the Village of Oak Creek, about 7 miles north of Interstate 17.

Hiking Instruction

Prescott College, an accredited, nationally recognized, four-year college, offers a diverse program in the liberal arts and the environment with on-campus and external B.A. and M.A. programs. Signature classes include month-long courses in rock climbing and mountaineering (taught by world-class climbers), kayaking, and wilderness travel. Prescott College, (800) 628-6364, www.prescott.edu/.

Friendly Pines Camp, an internationally known summer camp, offers Challenge programs for 6- to 13-year-olds. The multi-week programs include supervised camp and field instruction in hiking, overnight backpacking, and camp

opposite page:
Sedona's famous Cathedral Rock basks in the glow of a fiery sunset.
ROBERT G. McDONALD

skills. Their safety record is impeccable. Friendly Pines Camp, 933 Friendly Pines Road, Prescott, AZ 87303, (928) 445-2128.

Hiking Clubs & Programs

Here's a small sampling of Arizona contacts that focus on outdoor activities — sponsoring hikes, offering maps and newsletters, etc.

Statewide

Sierra Club
Grand Canyon Chapter
812 North Third Street, Phoenix, AZ 85004
(602) 253-8633
www.sierraclub.org/chapters/az/index.asp

Arizona Trail Association
P.O. Box 36736, Phoenix, AZ 85067-6736
(602) 252-4794; http://aztrail.org/

Arizona Trail Steward, Partnerships Division, Arizona State Parks, 1300 West Washington Street, Phoenix, AZ 85007; (602) 542-7120
www.pr.state.az.us/

Arizona Highways magazine
"Hike of the Month" feature
www.arizonahighways.com/
HikeofMonth/hike.html

Friends of Arizona Highways
2039 West Lewis Avenue, Phoenix, AZ 85009
(602) 712-2004
www.friendsofazhighways.com
This non-profit auxiliary of *Arizona Highways* magazine escorts a monthly hike (day hike or weekend outing) based on the "Hike of the Month" in *Arizona Highways*. Experienced escorts scout the route.

Arizona Public Lands Information Center
222 North Central Avenue, Phoenix, AZ 85004
(602) 417-9300

Metropolitan Phoenix

Arizona Outdoor and Travel Club
recorded hot line, (623) 931-0520

Backcountry Hiking Club
P.O. Box 27024, Tempe, AZ 85285
(480) 759-9279 or (480) 946-8991

Southern Arizona

Pima Trails Association
P.O. Box 41358, Tucson, AZ 85717
(520) 577-7979; www.pimatrails.org/

Southern Arizona Hiking Club
P.O. Box 32257, Tucson, AZ 85751
recording, (520) 751-4513
Has a link on www.arizonahiker.com/

Ramblers Hiking Club
UA Associated Student Activities
University of Arizona
(520) 621-8046
Huachuca Hiking Club
P.O. Box 3555
Sierra Vista, AZ 85636-3555
www.primenet.com/~tomheld/hhc.html

Northern Arizona

Flagstaff Hiking Club
P.O. Box 423
Flagstaff, AZ 86002

Museum of Northern Arizona
Education Department
3101 North Fort Valley Road
Flagstaff, AZ 86001
(928) 774-5211, Extension 220
Offers adventure excursions, day trips, expeditions in the Colorado Plateau region.

Reading

These references offer information too extensive to cover in one book. Some may be out of print, but they're worth finding in your local library.

Accidents in North American Mountaineering is an annual publication that analyzes mountain-climbing and travel-related accidents for that year. The lessons apply to wilderness travel in general. American Alpine Club, Golden, CO.

Along the Arizona Trail by M. John Fayhee is a coffee-table book on the Arizona Trail. The photographic portfolio features an informative narrative to give the reader a visual summary of the extent of the Arizona Trail. Westcliffe Publishers, 1998.

Arizona Natural Environment by Charles H. Lowe is a comprehensive introduction to Arizona's landscapes and habitats. University of Arizona Press, Tucson.

Arizona's Mogollon Rim: Travel Guide to Payson and Beyond by Don Dedera describes Mogollon Rim communities and many of the key hikes around them. *Arizona Highways* magazine, fourth printing, 2000.

Desert Survival is the most complete booklet on desert survival in Arizona — and it's free. Maricopa County Department of Civil Defense and Emergency Services, 2035 North 52nd Street, Phoenix, AZ 85008, (602) 273-1411.

Two Audubon Society nature guides — *Deserts* by James A. MacMahon and *Western Forests* by Stephen Whitney — are "must have" comprehensive references to wildflowers, trees, birds, reptiles, mammals, insects, and more. Alfred A. Knopf, New York.

Fit or Fat? A New Way to Health and Fitness Through Nutrition and Aerobic Exercise by Covert Bailey is excellent. Houghton Mifflin, Boston.

International Mountain Rescue Handbook by Hamish MacInnes gives graphic insight into the details and planning necessary to make a successful rescue. Charles Scribner's & Sons, New York.

Medicine for Mountaineering edited by James A. Wilkerson, M.D., is the recognized field source detailing the cause and field treatment of traumatic and environmental injuries and nontraumatic diseases. The Mountaineers, Seattle, WA.

Mountaineering: The Freedom of the Hills edited by Ed Peters is the most comprehensive source on mountain travel. The Mountaineers, Seattle, WA.

On the Arizona Trail: A Guide for Hikers, Cyclists, and Equestrians, by Kelly Tighe and Susan Moran, is a detailed guidebook describing the completed trail route so far and the interconnecting routes to get from one passage's end and the next passage's trailhead. Includes general travel guidelines for the terrain and climate encompassed by this massive trail system, trail steward contacts, and much practical information. Pruett Publishers, 1998.

Outdoor Survival Skills by Larry Dean Olsen is *the* source on primitive survival techniques by an author who has mastered them in the wilderness. Brigham Young University, Provo, UT.

Van Aaken Method by Ernst Van Aaken, M.D., is a top source on endurance running and travel, complemented with a non-nonsense approach to nutrition. World Publications, Mountain View, CA.

Venomous Animals of Arizona by Robert L. Smith is the guide to your worst nightmares. Read this, and chances are you'll avoid them in the field. Cooperative Extension Service, College of Agriculture, University of Arizona, Tucson, AZ 85721.

Walking Softly in the Wilderness by John Hart is probably the single best guide to backpacking. Sierra Club Books, San Francisco.

Weathering the Wilderness by William F. Reifsnyder is a practical guide to meteorology as it relates to wilderness travel. Sierra Club Books, San Francisco.

Maps

Arizona Public Lands Information Center
222 North Central Avenue
Phoenix, AZ 85004
(602) 417-9300

Arizona Trail Association
P.O. Box 36736
Phoenix, AZ 85067-6736
(602) 252-4794; http://aztrail.org/

Bureau of Land Management
Arizona State Office
222 North Central Avenue
Phoenix, AZ 85004
(602) 417-9200; www.az.blm.gov/

The Mogollon Rim Illustrated Camping/Hiking Guide. Fold-out map shows 20 trails in the Rim country, campground charts with RV information. *Arizona Highways* magazine, (602) 712-2000, (800) 543-5432
www.arizonahighways.com/

Pima Trails Association
P.O. Box 41358
Tucson, AZ 85717
(520) 577-7979; www.pimatrails.org/

Rainbow Expeditions trail and recreation maps from
Rainbow Expeditions Inc.
915 South Sherwood Village Drive
Tucson, AZ 85710
(520) 298-2731
Also available at the Summit Hut in Tucson.

U.S. Geological Survey topographical maps. Sold locally through commercial vendors, or order from:
USGS Information Services
P.O. Box 25286
Denver CO 80225
(888) 275-8747; www.ask.usgs.gov/

U.S. Forest Service
U.S. Department of Agriculture
Public Affairs Office
517 Gold Avenue
NW, Albuquerque, NM 87102
(505) 842-3292

Community Tourism
Information (listed by region)

Statewide

Arizona Office of Tourism
(888) 520-3434
www.arizonaguide.com

Northern Arizona & Grand Canyon

Flagstaff Convention and
Visitors Bureau
(928) 779-7611
www.flagstaff.az.us

Flagstaff Visitor Center
(800) 842-7293

Holbrook Chamber of Commerce
(928) 524-6558

Navajo Nation Tribal Government
Window Rock, AZ
(928) 871-6352

Navajo Parks and
Recreation Department
(928) 871-6647

Navajoland Tourism
(928) 871-6436

Page-Lake Powell Chamber
& Visitor Bureau
(888) 261-7243
www.visitlakepowell.com

Seligman Chamber of Commerce
(928) 422-3939

Sedona-Oak Creek Chamber of Commerce
(800) 288-7336
(928) 282-7722
www.sedonachamber.com

Winslow Chamber of Commerce
& Visitor Center
(928) 289-2434

Central Arizona

Camp Verde Chamber of Commerce
(928) 567-9294

Cottonwood/Verde Valley
Chamber of Commerce
(928) 634-7593

Jerome Chamber of Commerce
P.O. Drawer K,
Jerome, AZ 86331
(928) 634-2900, event recording/message
line; www.azjerome.com

Town of Jerome
(928) 634-7943

Greater Phoenix Convention
and Visitors Bureau
(602) 254-6500

Phoenix Chamber of Commerce
(602) 254-5521

Prescott Chamber Tourist Information Center
(800) 266-7534
(928) 445-2000
www.prescott.org

Rim Country Regional Chamber of Commerce
Payson office
(800) 672-9766
(928) 474-4515
Pine office
(928) 476-3547
www.rimcountrychamber.com

Western Arizona

Kingman Chamber of Commerce
(928) 753-6106

Powerhouse Visitor Center (Kingman area)
(928) 753-6132

Southern Arizona

Ajo Chamber of Commerce
(520) 387-7742

Douglas Chamber of Commerce
(520) 364-2477

Graham County Chamber of Commerce
(888) 837-1841
(520) 428-2511

Nogales-Santa Cruz County
Chamber of Commerce
(520) 287-3685

Patagonia Community Association
(520) 394-0060 or (888) 794-0060
www.theriver.com/public/patagoniaaz

Metropolitan Tucson Convention
and Visitor Bureau
(800) 638-8350

Willcox Chamber of Commerce
(800) 200-2272

Yuma County Convention
and Visitors Bureau
(520) 783-0071

index